Human Genetics

Other Books in the Current Controversies Series

Human Genetics

Noël Merino, Book Editor

GREENHAVEN PRESS
A part of Gale, Cengage Learning

Detroit • New York • San Francisco • New Haven, Conn • Waterville, Maine • London

Christine Nasso, *Publisher*
Elizabeth Des Chenes, *Managing Editor*

© 2010 Greenhaven Press, a part of Gale, Cengage Learning

Gale and Greenhaven Press are registered trademarks used herein under license.

For more information, contact:
Greenhaven Press
27500 Drake Rd.
Farmington Hills, MI 48331-3535
Or you can visit our Internet site at gale.cengage.com

For product information and technology assistance, contact us at

Gale Customer Support, 1-800-877-4253
For permission to use material from this text or product, submit all requests online at www.cengage.com/permissions

Further permissions questions can be emailed to permissionrequest@cengage.com

Articles in Greenhaven Press anthologies are often edited for length to meet page requirements. In addition, original titles of these works are changed to clearly present the main thesis and to explicitly indicate the author's opinion. Every effort is made to ensure that Greenhaven Press accurately reflects the original intent of the authors. Every effort has been made to trace the owners of copyrighted material.

Cover image copyright © Ann Johansson/Corbis.

LIBRARY OF CONGRESS CATALOGING-IN-PUBLICATION DATA

Human genetics / Noël Merino, book editor.
    p. cm. -- (Current controversies)
Includes bibliographical references and index.
    ISBN 978-0-7377-4707-2 (hardcover) -- ISBN 978-0-7377-4708-9 (pbk.)
1. Human genetics. I. Merino, Noël.
    QH431.H8356 2010
    174.2--dc22

                                                                2009048143

Printed in the United States of America
1 2 3 4 5 6 7 14 13 12 11 10

Contents

Chapter 2: What Are Some Concerns About Genetic Testing?

Chapter 3: Should People Be Free to Pursue Genetic Enhancement?

Yes: People Should Be Free to Pursue Genetic Enhancement

Chapter 4: Should Genes Be Available for Patent?

No: Genes Should Not Be Available for Patent

Foreword

By definition, controversies are "discussions of questions in which opposing opinions clash" (Webster's Twentieth Century Dictionary Unabridged). Few would deny that controversies are a pervasive part of the human condition and exist on virtually every level of human enterprise. Controversies transpire between individuals and among groups, within nations and between nations. Controversies supply the grist necessary for progress by providing challenges and challengers to the status quo. They also create atmospheres where strife and warfare can flourish. A world without controversies would be a peaceful world; but it also would be, by and large, static and prosaic.

The Series' Purpose

The purpose of the Current Controversies series is to explore many of the social, political, and economic controversies dominating the national and international scenes today. Titles selected for inclusion in the series are highly focused and specific. For example, from the larger category of criminal justice, Current Controversies deals with specific topics such as police brutality, gun control, white collar crime, and others. The debates in Current Controversies also are presented in a useful, timeless fashion. Articles and book excerpts included in each title are selected if they contribute valuable, long-range ideas to the overall debate. And wherever possible, current information is enhanced with historical documents and other relevant materials. Thus, while individual titles are current in focus, every effort is made to ensure that they will not become quickly outdated. Books in the Current Controversies series will remain important resources for librarians, teachers, and students for many years.

In addition to keeping the titles focused and specific, great care is taken in the editorial format of each book in the series. Book introductions and chapter prefaces are offered to provide background material for readers. Chapters are organized around several key questions that are answered with diverse opinions representing all points on the political spectrum. Materials in each chapter include opinions in which authors clearly disagree as well as alternative opinions in which authors may agree on a broader issue but disagree on the possible solutions. In this way, the content of each volume in Current Controversies mirrors the mosaic of opinions encountered in society. Readers will quickly realize that there are many viable answers to these complex issues. By questioning each author's conclusions, students and casual readers can begin to develop the critical thinking skills so important to evaluating opinionated material.

Current Controversies is also ideal for controlled research. Each anthology in the series is composed of primary sources taken from a wide gamut of informational categories including periodicals, newspapers, books, U.S. and foreign government documents, and the publications of private and public organizations. Readers will find factual support for reports, debates, and research papers covering all areas of important issues. In addition, an annotated table of contents, an index, a book and periodical bibliography, and a list of organizations to contact are included in each book to expedite further research.

Perhaps more than ever before in history, people are confronted with diverse and contradictory information. During the Persian Gulf War, for example, the public was not only treated to minute-to-minute coverage of the war, it was also inundated with critiques of the coverage and countless analyses of the factors motivating U.S. involvement. Being able to sort through the plethora of opinions accompanying today's major issues, and to draw one's own conclusions, can be a complicated and frustrating struggle. It is the editors' hope that Current Controversies will help readers with this struggle.

Introduction

"Genetic research, in general, has spawned great concern, but the issue of how it may be used outside of treating and preventing disease continues to be especially controversial."

Scientific knowledge about human genetics has been rapidly advancing over the last few decades. With advancing knowledge about human genetics comes the ability to radically change the way humans deal with disease: Genetic research has already led to certain genetic tests that give information about disease and to experimentation with gene therapy to treat disease. In addition to its application to disease, the advancing genetic knowledge could allow human beings the opportunity to profoundly alter their genetics for other purposes beyond health. Genetic research, in general, has spawned great concern, but the issue of how it may be used outside of treating and preventing disease continues to be especially controversial.

Genetic testing is one technology resulting from recent research into human genetics. The field of genetic testing is still in its infancy and the potential of such technology is still largely debated. Blood tests are available for over one thousand diseases, but the results only tell people whether they carry a particular gene correlated with a particular disease. The extent to which other factors affect this propensity for certain diseases is unknown, making the usefulness of the tests themselves questionable. As journalist Claudia Kalb wrote in the December 11, 2006, issue of *Newsweek*, "Scientific revolutions must be tempered by reality. Genes aren't the only factors involved in complex diseases—lifestyle and environmental influences such as diet or smoking are too." Genetic testing may or may not ultimately be seen as progress in the prevention and treatment of human disease, but it currently holds that promise. Given the limited knowledge testing confers at the present time, there are competing views about whether or not such testing is beneficial, in light of other concerns.

Another area of human genetics research that holds promise for the prevention of and treatment of disease is gene therapy. Gene therapy includes the replacement of genes, the inactivation of genes, and the insertion of new genes. This kind of therapy is still in the experimental stage and the experiments are controversial because of the risks associated with gene therapy. Eighteen-year-old Jesse Gelsinger died in 1999 during a gene therapy clinical trial for the treatment of ornithine transcarbamylase (OTC) deficiency, a defect in the liver that causes the body to be unable to clear ammonia from the bloodstream. Even with the risks, gene therapy for diseases—especially those that are otherwise fatal—holds promise in the field of medicine. But disease is not the only potential purpose for gene therapy.

Within the field of human genetics research, probably the area of the most controversy and conjecture is the use of gene therapy for human enhancement. Speculation about uses of gene therapy outside of disease prevention and disease treatment abounds. Such speculation is especially popular within science fiction entertainment: The television show *Dark Angel* has many examples of possible future uses of gene therapy including the genetically enhanced main character, Max Guevara. Michael Crichton's *Next* is a fictional thriller about a researcher who mixes human genetic material with chimpanzee genetic material to create a hybrid being. If gene therapy becomes a viable procedure, the application beyond treatment and prevention of disease could be extensive. This area of future human genetics research has many proponents ready to step up and try new enhancement procedures, and numerous detractors concerned about the possibility of such things as genetic warfare and eugenics.

Human genetics is currently a hot topic. The research and application into genetic technologies is still in its infancy, and there is as much excitement as there is fear about what the future might bring. Although much of the research currently focuses on the use of genetic technologies such as genetic testing and gene therapy for disease prevention and treatment, there is no doubt that as the technology moves forward, other uses for the technology will be pursued. The current debates about the new genetic technologies—including genetic testing and gene therapy—are explored in *Current Controversies: Human Genetics*, shedding light on this fascinating and complicated contemporary issue.

CHAPTER 1

What Are Some Concerns About Genetic Research and Technology?

Overview: Human Genome Research

U.S. Department of Energy Office of Science

The U.S. Department of Energy Office of Science is the single largest supporter of basic research in the physical sciences in the United States.

Cells are the fundamental working units of every living system. All the instructions needed to direct their activities are contained within the chemical DNA (deoxyribonucleic acid).

DNA from all organisms is made up of the same chemical and physical components. The DNA sequence is the particular side-by-side arrangement of bases along the DNA strand (e.g., ATTCCGGA). This order spells out the exact instructions required to create a particular organism with its own unique traits.

The Human Genome

The genome is an organism's complete set of DNA. Genomes vary widely in size: The smallest known genome for a free-living organism (a bacterium) contains about 600,000 DNA base pairs, while human and mouse genomes have some 3 billion. Except for mature red blood cells, all human cells contain a complete genome.

DNA in each human cell is packaged into 46 chromosomes arranged into 23 pairs. Each chromosome is a physically separate molecule of DNA that ranges in length from about 50 million to 250 million base pairs. A few types of major chromosomal abnormalities, including missing or extra copies or gross breaks and rejoinings (translocations), can be

"Genomics and Its Impact on Science and Society: The Human Genome Project and Beyond," in U.S. Department of Energy Office of Science, June 2008, pp. 1–2, 5–6.

detected by microscopic examination. Most changes in DNA, however, are more subtle and require a closer analysis of the DNA molecule to find perhaps single-base differences.

Each chromosome contains many genes, the basic physical and functional units of heredity. Genes are specific sequences of bases that encode instructions on how to make proteins. Genes comprise only about 2% of the human genome; the remainder consists of noncoding regions, whose functions may include providing chromosomal structural integrity and regulating where, when, and in what quantity proteins are made. The human genome is estimated to contain some 25,000 genes.

The Proteome

Although genes get a lot of attention, the proteins perform most life functions and even comprise the majority of cellular structures. Proteins are large, complex molecules made up of chains of small chemical compounds called amino acids. Chemical properties that distinguish the 20 different amino acids cause the protein chains to fold up into specific three-dimensional structures that define their particular functions in the cell.

The Human Genome Project (HGP) traces its roots to an initiative in the U.S. Department of Energy (DOE).

The constellation of all proteins in a cell is called its proteome. Unlike the relatively unchanging genome, the dynamic proteome changes from minute to minute in response to tens of thousands of intra- and extracellular environmental signals. A protein's chemistry and behavior are determined by the gene sequence and by the number and identities of other proteins made in the same cell at the same time and with which it associates and reacts. Studies to explore protein structure and activities, known as proteomics, will be the focus of much research for decades to come and will help elucidate the molecular basis of health and disease.

The Human Genome Project

Though surprising to many, the Human Genome Project (HGP) traces its roots to an initiative in the U.S. Department of Energy (DOE). Since 1947, DOE and its predecessor agencies have been charged by Congress with developing new energy resources and technologies and pursuing a deeper understanding of potential health and environmental risks posed by their production and use. Such studies, for example, have provided the scientific basis for individual risk assessments of nuclear medicine technologies.

The human genome reference sequence provides a magnificent and unprecedented biological resource that will serve throughout the century as a basis for research and discovery.

In 1986, DOE took a bold step in announcing the Human Genome Initiative, convinced that its missions would be well served by a reference human genome sequence. Shortly thereafter, DOE joined with the National Institutes of Health [NIH] to develop a plan for a joint HGP that officially began in 1990. During the early years of the HGP, the Wellcome Trust, a private charitable institution in the United Kingdom, joined the effort as a major partner. Important contributions also came from other collaborators around the world, including Japan, France, Germany, and China.

The HGP's ultimate goal was to generate a high-quality reference DNA sequence for the human genome's 3 billion base pairs and to identify all human genes. Other important goals included sequencing the genomes of model organisms to interpret human DNA, enhancing computational resources to support future research and commercial applications, exploring gene function through mouse-human comparisons, studying human variation, and training future scientists in genomics.

The powerful analytical technology and data arising from the HGP present complex ethical and policy issues for individuals and society. These challenges include privacy, fairness in use and access of genomic information, reproductive and clinical issues, and commercialization. Programs that identify and address these implications have been an integral part of the HGP and have become a model for bioethics programs worldwide.

A Lasting Legacy

In June 2000, to much excitement and fanfare, scientists announced the completion of the first working draft of the entire human genome. First analyses of the details appeared in the February 2001 issues of the journals *Nature* and *Science*. The high-quality reference sequence was completed in April 2003, marking the end of the Human Genome Project—2 years ahead of the original schedule. Coincidentally, it also was the 50th anniversary of [American scientist James D.] Watson and [British scientist Francis] Crick's publication of DNA structure that launched the era of molecular biology.

Available to researchers worldwide, the human genome reference sequence provides a magnificent and unprecedented biological resource that will serve throughout the century as a basis for research and discovery and, ultimately, myriad practical applications. The sequence already is having an impact on finding genes associated with human disease. Hundreds of other genome sequence projects—on microbes, plants, and animals—have been completed since the inception of the HGP, and these data now enable detailed comparisons among organisms including humans.

Many more sequencing projects are under way or planned because of the research value of DNA sequence, the tremendous sequencing capacity now available, and continued improvements in technologies. Sequencing projects on the genomes of many microbes, as well as the chimpanzee, pig, sheep, and domestic cat, are in progress.

Beyond sequencing, growing areas of research focus on identifying important elements in the DNA sequence responsible for regulating cellular functions and providing the basis of human variation. Perhaps the most daunting challenge is to begin to understand how all the "parts" of cells—genes, proteins, and many other molecules—work together to create complex living organisms. Future analyses of this treasury of data will provide a deeper and more comprehensive understanding of the molecular processes underlying life and will have an enduring and profound impact on how we view our own place in it. . . .

Genetic Testing

DNA underlies almost every aspect of human health, both in function and dysfunction. Obtaining a detailed picture of how genes and other DNA sequences work together and interact with environmental factors ultimately will lead to the discovery of pathways involved in normal processes and in disease pathogenesis. Such knowledge will have a profound impact on the way disorders are diagnosed, treated, and prevented and will bring about revolutionary changes in clinical and public health practice. Some of these transformative developments are described below.

DNA-based tests are among the first commercial medical applications of the new genetic discoveries. Gene tests can be used to diagnose and confirm disease, even in asymptomatic individuals; provide prognostic information about the course of disease; and, with varying degrees of accuracy, predict the risk of future disease in healthy individuals or their progeny.

Currently, several hundred genetic tests are in clinical use, with many more under development, and their numbers and varieties are expected to increase rapidly over the next decade. Most current tests detect mutations associated with rare genetic disorders that follow Mendelian inheritance patterns. These include myotonic and Duchenne muscular dystrophies, cystic fibrosis, neurofibromatosis type 1, sickle-cell anemia, and Huntington's disease.

Recently, tests have been developed to detect mutations for a handful of more complex conditions such as breast, ovarian, and colon cancers. Although they have limitations, these tests sometimes are used to make risk estimates in presymptomatic individuals with a family history of the disorder. One potential benefit to these gene tests is that they could provide information to help physicians and patients manage the disease or condition more effectively. Regular colonoscopies for those having mutations associated with colon cancer, for instance, could prevent thousands of deaths each year.

Scientific Limitations

Some scientific limitations are that the tests may not detect every mutation associated with a particular condition (many are as yet undiscovered), and the ones they do detect may present different risks to various people and populations. Another important consideration in gene testing is the lack of effective treatments or preventive measures for many diseases and conditions now being diagnosed or predicted.

Knowledge about the risk of potential future disease can produce significant emotional and psychological impacts. Because genetic tests reveal information about individuals and their families, test results can affect family dynamics. Results also can pose risks for population groups if they lead to group stigmatization.

Other issues related to gene tests include their effective introduction into clinical practice, the regulation of laboratory quality assurance, the availability of testing for rare diseases, and the education of health care providers and patients about correct interpretation and attendant risks.

Families and individuals who have genetic disorders or are at risk for them often seek help from medical geneticists (an MD specialty) and genetic counselors (graduate degree training). These professionals can diagnose and explain disorders, review available options for testing and treatment, and provide emotional support.

Pharmacogenomics

Within the next decade, researchers will begin to correlate DNA variants with individual responses to medical treatments, identify particular subgroups of patients, and develop drugs customized for those populations. The discipline that blends pharmacology with genomic capabilities is called pharmacogenomics.

The potential for using genes themselves to treat disease or enhance particular traits has captured the imagination of the public and the biomedical community.

More than 100,000 people die each year from adverse responses to medications that may be beneficial to others. Another 2.2 million experience serious reactions, while others fail to respond at all. DNA variants in genes involved in drug metabolism, particularly the cytochrome P450 multigene family, are the focus of much current research in this area. Enzymes encoded by these genes are responsible for metabolizing most drugs used today, including many for treating psychiatric, neurological, and cardiovascular diseases. Enzyme function affects patient responses to both the drug and the dose. Future advances will enable rapid testing to determine the patient's genotype and guide treatment with the most effective drugs, in addition to drastically reducing adverse reactions.

Genomic data and technologies also are expected to make drug development faster, cheaper, and more effective. Most drugs today are based on about 500 molecular targets, but genomic knowledge of genes involved in diseases, disease pathways, and drug-response sites will lead to the discovery of thousands of additional targets. New drugs, aimed at specific sites in the body and at particular biochemical events leading to disease, probably will cause fewer side effects than many current medicines. Ideally, genomic drugs could be given earlier in the disease process. As knowledge becomes available to select patients most likely to benefit from a potential drug, pharmacogenomics will speed the design of clinical trials to market the drugs sooner.

Genetic Enhancement

The potential for using genes themselves to treat disease or enhance particular traits has captured the imagination of the public and the biomedical community. This largely experimental field—gene transfer or gene therapy—holds potential for treating or even curing such genetic and acquired diseases as cancers and AIDS by using normal genes to supplement or replace defective genes or to bolster a normal function such as immunity.

Almost 1,200 clinical gene therapy trials were identified worldwide in 2006. The majority (67%) take place in the United States, followed by Europe (29%). Although most trials focus on various types of cancer, studies also involve other multigenic and monogenic, infectious, and vascular diseases. Most current protocols are aimed at establishing the safety of gene-delivery procedures rather than effectiveness.

Gene transfer still faces many scientific obstacles before it can become a practical approach for treating disease. According to the American Society of Human Genetics' "Statement on Gene Therapy," effective progress will be achieved only through continued rigorous research on the most fundamental mechanisms underlying gene delivery and gene expression in animals.

Human Genetic Knowledge Will Give Us Benefits and Burdens

Eric Cohen

Eric Cohen is an adjunct fellow at the Ethics and Public Policy Center and editor-at-large of the New Atlantis.

L ooking at where the science of genetics is heading, we must beware the twin vices of overprediction and under-prediction. Overprediction risks blinding us to the significance of present realities, by inebriating us with distant dreams and distant nightmares. Under-prediction risks blinding us to where today's technological breakthroughs may lead, both for better and for worse. Prediction requires the right kind of caution—caution about letting our imaginations run wild, and caution about letting science proceed without limits, be-cause we falsely assume that it is always innocent and always will be. To think clearly, therefore, we must put aside the grand dreams and great nightmares of the genetic future to consider the moral meaning of the genetic present—the mean-ing of what we can do now and why we do it. And we need to explore what these new genetic possibilities might mean for how we live, what we value, and how we treat one another.

Humanly speaking, the new genetics seems to have five di-mensions or meanings: (1) genetics as a route to self-understanding, a way of knowing ourselves; (2) genetics as a route to new medical therapies, a way of curing ourselves; (3) genetics as a potential tool for human re-engineering, a pros-pect I find far-fetched; (4) genetics as a means of knowing something about our biological destiny, about our health and sickness in the future; and (5) genetics as a tool for screening the traits of the next generation, for choosing some lives and rejecting others. I want to explore each of these five dimensions in turn—beginning with the hunger for self-understanding.

Genetic Self-Understanding

The first reason for engaging in modern genetics is simply man's desire to know himself, a desire that nearly all of us share, if not in equal degrees. Alone among the animals, human beings possess the capacity and the drive to look upon ourselves as objects of inquiry. We study ourselves because we are not content simply being ourselves. We are not satisfied living immediately in nature like the other animals do. Food and sex alone do not satiate us. We do not accept the given world as it is; we also seek to uncover its meaning and structure. Modern biology, of course, is only one avenue of self-understanding, one way of asking questions. But it is an especially powerful and prominent way of seeking self-knowledge in the modern age. Instead of asking who we are by exploring how humans live, the biologist asks who we are by examining the mechanics of human life. Genetics fits perfectly within this vision: it seems to offer us a code for life; it promises to shed empirical light on our place in nature; it claims to tell us something reliable about our *human* design, our *prehuman* origins, and our *post-human* fate.

The triumph of modern genetics has also meant the humbling of modern genetics.

But it is also true that the more we learn about genetics, the more we seem to confront the limits as well as the significance of genetic explanation. As the cell biologist Lenny Moss put it:

Once upon a time it was believed that something called "genes" were integral units, that each specified a piece of phenotype, that the phenotype as a whole was the result of the sum of these units, and that evolutionary change was the result of new changes created by random mutation and differential survival. Once upon a time it was believed that the chromosomal location of genes was irrelevant, that DNA was the citadel of stability, that DNA which didn't code for proteins was biological "junk," and that coding DNA included, as it were, its own instructions for use. Once upon a time it would have stood to reason that the complexity of an organism would be proportional to the number of its unique genetic units.

Modern Genetics

But in fact, the triumph of modern genetics has also meant the humbling of modern genetics. Big hypotheses now seem to require revision and greater measure. And in many ways, we are probably relieved that genetics does not tell us everything we need to know about ourselves. For human beings, this means that we are still more free than any genetic account of being human would leave us. And for young scientists, this means that life's mystery is still as great as ever; today's earnest graduate student can surpass even [American scientist James D.] Watson and [British scientist Francis] Crick in making the crucial breakthrough that might reveal our humanity once and for all—that might give us "the secret of life," as Crick declared when he burst into the British pub in 1953.

Even as we are relieved at discovering the limits of genetic determinism, however, our hunger for genetic explanation remains strong. Disease is also a threat to our freedom, after all, and we still hope that genetics might help us conquer that mortal threat. We still hope that genetics is the secret of disease, if not the secret of life.

Genetic Therapy

And this leads me to the second dimension of the new genetics: the search for medical cures. Modern science, unlike ancient science, does not rest on the foundation of curiosity alone. It seeks to conquer nature, not simply to understand nature's meaning. And while man may be the only truly curious animal, his curiosity is not his only guiding passion. He also seeks health and he certainly fears death. Like other animals, human beings seek comfort and survival. But unlike other animals, we possess the capacity to pursue comfort and survival through the systematic application of reason. Modern science, especially modern biology, promises the "relief of man's estate," in [English philosopher] Francis Bacon's famous phrase, in return for the right to explore nature without limits. [French philosopher René] Descartes skillfully negotiated this bargain centuries ago, and I quote here a passage much cited by those interested in the origins of modern science:

> So soon as I had acquired some general notions concerning physics ... they caused me to see that it is possible to attain knowledge which is very useful for life, and that, instead of that speculative philosophy which is found in the schools, we may find a practical philosophy by means of which, knowing the force and the action of fire, water, air, the stars, heaven, and all the other bodies that environ us, as distinctly as we know the different crafts of our artisans, we can in the same way employ them in all those uses to which they are adapted, and thus render ourselves as the masters and possessors of nature.

Not surprisingly, the "nature" we most seek to "master" is our own. We seek to conquer human disease, and perhaps even to make death itself a series of conquerable diseases. It is apparently part of our genetic code to revolt against our genetic fate.

Of course, the "speculative philosophy" of the schools that Descartes sought to leave behind was religious metaphysics— which is to say, the search for man's place in the cosmological whole and before God. The new science and the old religion thus seem to present us with two different ways of revolting against our biological fate: The religious believer seeks such revolt *beyond nature* in God, by looking beyond our genetic deficiencies to the hope of eternal salvation. The scientist seeks such revolt *through nature* in science, by understanding nature's mishaps (or mutations) so that we might correct them. The unknowable God, if you believe He really exists, promises better long-term results; He "cures" us forever, but only after death. The empirical scientist, if you give him enough public funding, provides better short-term results; he cures us now, but only for a while. This does not mean that science and religion are enemies: Religious people are often great scientists, and great scientists are often deeply religious. But it does suggest that the cure-seeking scientist lives on the narrow ridge between holiness and rebellion: He imitates the old God by healing the sick; or he supplants the old God by believing that he can eradicate all sickness, by working within nature rather than looking beyond it.

Most diseases are more complicated than genetics alone.

A New Frontier

Genetics, in this sense, is simply a new frontier in the long ascent of modern medicine. It aims to repair broken genes or correct disease-causing mutations by direct intervention. And it aims to use our growing understanding of the human genome to diagnose and treat human disease with greater precision.

But it turns out that most diseases are more complicated than genetics alone, and that markers for identifying and predicting a given disease do not always or easily translate into usable knowledge about the disease's causation. The capacity to fix genes with perfect precision and without side effects is also proving remarkably difficult. Already, there have been some high-profile examples of gene-therapy trials going terribly wrong, and the field now proceeds with perhaps a more befitting caution. Over time, of course, there is little doubt that our genetic knowledge will improve modern medicine and thus prove a great blessing to us all. But there also seems little doubt that the new genetics will probably not be the therapeutic panacea that many once hoped, and which many scientists and policy makers offered as a central justification for the Human Genome Project. Biological knowledge and biological control are simply not the same, even when it comes to curing disease, and most certainly when it comes to so-called genetic engineering.

Genetic Design

This brings me to the third dimension of the new genetics: the much-discussed prospect of designing our descendants—a prospect I find unlikely. In the reproductive context, I think the real dilemma may involve picking and choosing human embryos for implantation based on the genetic characteristics that nature gave them. But this is significantly different from designing human beings with genotypes entirely of our own creation. By focusing so much energy on the dream and the nightmare of genetic engineering, we risk treating the real-life possibilities of genetic control as less profound than they really are. Yet again: We worry too much too early or too little too late.

To be sure, it may be possible to engineer various genetic monstrosities—like a human version of the monkeys with jellyfish genes that glow in the dark. Perhaps some modern-day Frankenstein will create fetuses with primordial wings; or children with seven fingers; or human beings that are part male and part female by design. If human life is seen as a mere canvas, and if the biologist sees himself as an artist thriving on "transgression," then genetic engineering is a real problem. And sadly, there is little doubt that someone, somewhere, will attempt such terrible experiments, and may succeed in producing at least embryonic or fetal monsters. But I also have little doubt that most democratic societies will pass laws that prohibit the biological equivalent of postmodern art. Precisely because it is so grotesque, such monster-making is not our most serious ethical problem.

We need to pay much closer attention to the human meaning of genetic knowledge *itself—both how we use it and what it does to us once we possess it.*

Democratic societies, after all, do not seek the monstrous; we seek the useful. And the worst abuses of biotechnology may come in trying to make the seemingly monstrous dimensions of life disappear in the name of mercy, by screening and aborting those with handicaps or deformities that we believe make their lives not worth living. There will always be knaves who reject society's laws and principles and engage in monstrous acts for their own sake. But the real challenge is to consider those uses of genetic knowledge and genetic choice that are both technically feasible (as science, not art) and that seem to run with rather than against the grain of liberal society. It is those potential abuses that have some utilitarian justification—such as improving life, or ending suffering, or guaranteeing every child a healthy genome, or expanding reproductive freedom—that we must confront most squarely....

Genetic Foreknowledge

But if most forms of genetic engineering, beyond cloning, are probably not in the offing, this hardly means that the new genetics is socially and ethically insignificant. Certainly not. What it means is that we need to pay much closer attention to the human meaning of *genetic knowledge* itself—both how we use it and what it does to us once we possess it. And this brings me to the fourth dimension of the new genetics: the meaning of gaining partial foreknowledge about our biological fate, and especially the meaning of knowing bad things (or good things) about our biological future. . . .

Right now, the number of diseases we can test for genetically is somewhat limited, and many of these tests offer clear positive or negative diagnoses. But what may be coming is a world of imperfect knowledge about terrible possibilities— with a battery of tests that give greater and lesser probabilities of getting certain diseases, at certain times, compared to the general population. All of our human fears will be sharpened; our paranoia made more precise; our anxieties given a genetic scorecard. What good is this knowledge to us, especially when the power to diagnose will come long before the power to cure—the so-called "diagnostic-therapeutic gap"? And yet, will we be able to resist this new form of high-tech astrology? Will it teach us to number our days and make us wise? Or will it make life seem like a short trip through a genetic minefield— by forcing us to confront every morning the ways we might die?

The pursuit of genetic equality will lead to the age of genetic discrimination.

Genetic Choice

These types of genetic foreknowledge take on new meaning when we move to the reproductive sphere, and when the burden is not simply living with knowledge of one's own potential fate, but deciding whether such knowledge is a morally compelling reason to abort an affected fetus or discard an affected embryo. And this leads us to the final dimension of the new genetics: the use of genetic knowledge to make reproductive decisions, to decide between life worth living and life unworthy of life.

For a long time, we have worried about the so-called "enhancement problem," and feared that some people would use genetic technology to get an unfair advantage for their offspring. But this, I believe, is the wrong worry. The real danger is that the limitless pursuit of equal results—the desire to give everyone a mutation-free life, and thus an equal chance at the pursuit of happiness—will actually undermine our belief in the intrinsic equality of all persons. The pursuit of genetic equality will lead to the age of genetic discrimination. And in some ways, it already has. . . .

Beyond Genetics

Without question, the advance of modern genetics is one of the great achievements of our time, an example of the creative and truth-seeking spirit at the heart of our humanity. But too often, we easily assume that the progress of science is identical to the progress of man. The truth, as always, is much more complicated. Many men and women of the past were superior in virtue to us now, and many scientific discoveries of the present and future will prove a mixed blessing, and sometimes even a curse.

The new genetics will deliver us many goods but also confront us with many burdens. We will need to make choices, and those choices will require philosophical judgments about "better" and "worse," not only scientific judgments about "possible" and "impossible." We will need to think especially about the goods in life that are higher than health—the goods that make being healthy worthwhile. And this is the very task that modern genetics is least equipped to handle.

We will also need to challenge the lazy assumption that genetic knowledge is simply "neutral," with a meaning that depends entirely on "how we use it." For this, too, is much too simple. New knowledge is never neutral; it is always a way of being in the world, a way of seeing our condition, a way of seeking truth, happiness, and virtue. Genetics is no exception, and genetic knowledge will never eradicate or eliminate those perplexities of life that require the kind of wisdom that no material science can ever offer.

The Future of Genetic Technology Needs to Be Controlled

Richard Hayes

Richard Hayes is executive director of the Center for Genetics and Society, an organization working to encourage responsible use of the new human genetic technologies.

Most of us would enjoy being healthier, smarter, more attractive, and longer-lived. But we also know there can be too much of a good thing. If we're overweight it makes sense to reduce, but anorexia can be lethal. A nice haircut can make us feel good, but repeated, expensive cosmetic surgery can bring more complications than compliments. Most of us understand this and learn to lead full and productive lives within the natural range of diversity that comes with being human.

But what if that natural range of diversity no longer applied? What if it were possible to radically enhance our looks, brains, athletic abilities, and life span with, say, injections of customized genes? What if we could design our children with chromosomes purchased from a catalogue? . . .

Four Biopolitical Scenarios

The four scenarios of the human biopolitical future presented below may help us think through these issues. They take place over the 15-year period from 2007 through 2021.

A central theme is the tension between libertarian and communitarian values. Humans evolved with tendencies both to compete and to cooperate, and societies have varied in the

Richard Hayes, "Our Biopolitical Future: Four Scenarios," *World Watch*, vol. 20, March-April 2007, pp. 10–17. Copyright © 2007. www.worldwatch.org. Reproduced by permission.

emphasis they give to one tendency or the other. Environmentalists are familiar with the libertarian/communitarian tension as *the tragedy of the commons*: An individual may benefit by polluting a river or the atmosphere, but if everyone seeks to benefit in this manner everyone suffers. . . .

It's unlikely that the future will play out precisely as sketched in any one of these scenarios. But there *will* be a future. The more we are clear about those futures we wish to avoid and those we would welcome, the easier it will be to figure out what we are called to do now.

Scenario One: Libertarian Transhumanism Triumphs

The opening years of the 21st century were marked by controversy over cloning, stem cells, and human genetic modification. Despite concern about fraudulent cloning claims and unethical gene therapy experiments, genetic technology was increasingly seen as part of a progressive vision that rejected outworn, traditionalist values and embraced a bright future of technological innovation and economic growth.

Among the earliest adopters of genetic modification were athletes, and the public turned out in droves to see gene-doped competitors break one record after another.

During this same period libertarian sentiment grew rapidly among many Americans, encouraged by a well-funded network of think tanks, bloggers, and entrepreneurial scientists. By 2009 their ideology of "free markets, free choice, free bodies," was spreading at the expense of both religious conservativism and social democratic liberalism. Democrats and Republicans alike argued in favor of free trade, school vouchers, deregulation, privatization, personal retirement accounts, pharmacological freedom, and reprogenetic autonomy.

With visions of trillion-dollar markets waiting to be served, global biotech conglomerates raced to develop technologies allowing parents to screen embryos for behavioral and cosmetic traits. For the other end of the life cycle, these same firms established high-tech life-extension and cryonics facilities throughout the world, most lucratively in small countries proudly advertising their lack of regulatory oversight.

Among the earliest adopters of genetic modification were athletes, and the public turned out in droves to see gene-doped competitors break one record after another. Despite hand-wringing from an older generation of sports professionals and a short-lived protest movement by concerned parents, by 2011 athletics was fast becoming a contest of competing genetic interventions rather than innate ability, coaching, and practice.

The End of the Natural

A major threshold was crossed in 2013, when Swedish scientists announced the birth of the first true "designer baby," that is, a child able to pass its modified genes to its own children. Although ostensibly developed to prevent congenital disease, within four years the procedure was being offered commercially for a wide range of aesthetic, cognitive, and performance enhancements. The cost of a designer baby was high (about US$235,000), but affluent couples flocked to the new "better baby" clinics to ensure that their children had the best genes money could buy.

"Techno" has fully replaced "natural" as a hallmark of excellence.

Meanwhile the transhumanist movement, which had started as a fringe group of sci-fi cultists in Los Angeles in the early 1990s, was growing into a major social force. The transhumanists were obsessed with the prospect of reconfiguring the human species and the rest of the natural world through genetic modification, nanotechnology, and synthetic biology. The combination of libertarian politics and transhumanism resonated strongly with ambitious young technophiles throughout the world, and an increasing number of up-and-coming figures in the sciences, commerce, the arts, and politics openly identified themselves as libertarian trans-humanists. . . .

Now, in 2021, it's clear that there's no going back. "Techno" has fully replaced "natural" as a hallmark of excellence. The genetically enhanced elites relax in their gated communities, dine on transgenic squash and cloned beef, dote on their cloned pets, and look forward to receiving the latest GenePak® uploads for their kids. Libertarian transhumanism has become the hegemonic vision of the human future. Few people can any longer imagine a credible alternative.

Scenario Two: One Family, One Future

The opening years of the 21st century were marked by controversy over cloning, stem cells, and human genetic modification. In 2008 the U.S. biotech industry organized a political action committee to promote an industry-friendly agenda of "Cures for All." Initial success was tarnished, however, when covert human cloning labs were discovered the following year in Thailand. Embryos used for these illicit experiments were traced to fertility clinics associated with the World Stem Cell Consortium, established by scientists in Australia, Belize, and Cyprus, to help themselves and others evade national regulations.

In 2010 a German human rights group documented the deaths of over 300 women worldwide from ovarian hyper-stimulation syndrome, the result of aggressive efforts to obtain eggs for cloning research. Meanwhile wealthy individuals were increasingly outsourcing the entire process of reproduction. Women rated "Grade A" were routinely being offered sums in excess of US$150,000 for their eggs, genetically "superior" sperm could be purchased over the Internet, and young women from Ukraine and Romania were paid little better than minimum wage for the use of their wombs. In 2012 a Scottish gene therapy experiment gone awry left two dozen infants with an incurable form of bone cancer and life expectancies of less than 12 years.

Religious conservatives saw an opening, and began speaking out against the eugenic juggernaut and in support of equality, social justice, human rights, women's and children's health, the sanctity of the natural world, and the precautionary principle. The political tide began to shift. After winning filibuster-proof congressional majorities in the United States in 2014, conservatives quickly succeeded in banning reproductive and research cloning, sex selection, research using human/animal chimeras, physician-assisted suicide, child-accessible Internet pornography, and gas-guzzling SUVs. Protests were heard from the biotech industry, civil libertarians, and the automakers, but the great majority of people in the United States were relieved to find that someone was finally willing to draw some lines.

The Rise of Neo-Traditionalism

During these same years, growing repugnance over the dehumanizing impacts of the new genetic technologies, technocapitalist globalization, and the pervasive tawdriness and superficiality of the postmodern world helped fuel neo-traditionalist movements in Europe, Asia, Africa, and the Americas. The gifted German-Turkish writer Fredericka Musfika, author of the influential book *Humanity or Transhumanity?*, drew on conservative Islamic, Christian, Jewish, Hindu, and Confucian social values to offer a universalist vision of a human future embracing peace, love, and harmony with nature. Her impassioned speaking and writing gave rise to the mass social movement known as "One Family, One Future"

(OFOF). It was a secular movement open to people of any (or no) religious faith, but it adopted codes of conduct similar to those found in many traditional religions. In the period after 2016 the practice of wearing a full-length woolen scarf displaying OFOF iconography spread throughout the world as a symbol of the rejection of postmodernity.

Although OFOF endorsed the use of the Supernet, the iWeb, and other new information technologies, it viewed high-tech medical practices with suspicion. By 2018 many countries had abandoned research on genetic modification. The use of naturopathy, aroma therapy, herbal preparatories, and a form of massage therapy accompanied by poetry and song had all but replaced conventional medical treatment among significant sectors of the world's population.

As early as 2017 the established religious denominations began losing members to OFOF. In some North American and European cities as much as 30 percent of the population would gather for OFOF's Saturday affirmation services. This proportion is certain to increase, because OFOF families shun birth control and now average seven children per couple.

In 2019 OFOF-USA announced the formation of a political party, and in last year's (2020) elections OFOF candidates—all men, and all wearing the full, luxuriant beards that now designate OFOF clan leaders—won two dozen seats in the House and four in the Senate, taking votes from both Republicans and Democrats. Similar parliamentary gains have been made in about 20 other countries. Earlier this year, OFOF leaders told the tens of thousands gathered at their 2021 annual World Convocation that the human future never looked as promising as it does today.

Scenario Three: A Techno-Eugenic Arms Race

The opening years of the 21st century were marked by controversy over cloning, stem cells, and human genetic modification. In 2008 biotech enthusiasts in the United States organized a national campaign to "liberate" stem cell research by loosening even the minimal existing state and federal oversight guidelines. Although many scientists worried that this would allow ethically questionable activities to be swept under the carpet, they were reluctant to break ranks and speak out for fear of giving aid and comfort to demands by the religious right that stem cell research be banned entirely.

A new techno-eugenic arms race rapidly escalated out of control.

In 2010 North Korean scientists announced the birth of a child genetically modified to allow an increased respiratory capacity of 18 percent above the human norm. The scientists involved made no pretense that this was done to address a medical need. Rather, they said, it was the first step toward creating "The New Man" for the 21st century.

Just eight months later, China—with an exploding GDP [gross domestic product], growing nationalist fervor, and 60,000 freshly trained biotech engineers entering the workforce each year—announced a national initiative to improve the genetic quality of its people. All couples at risk of transmitting genes identified as deleterious were required to take steps to avoid doing so, with the government covering all costs. In addition, couples could volunteer to have their children "enhanced," again with all costs covered. Leading Chinese rock stars and taikonauts [space travelers from China] were featured in a massive media campaign promoting the program.

Alarms were raised by international human rights and social justice organizations, but to little effect. Other countries knew they had to follow China's lead or risk having their children left behind. A new techno-eugenic arms race rapidly escalated out of control.

A Post-Human Future

In 2014 the CIA [Central Intelligence Agency] reported that Venezuelan scientists had created a virus that turned skin cells containing specified concentrations of melanin carcinogenic. Other countries enacted laws requiring the medical termination of "lives not worth living." Still others approved forms of human experimentation, using prisoners, the disabled, terminally ill patients, orphans, and others, that had been anathema barely a decade earlier. . . .

The field was increasingly dominated by dismissively arrogant scientists, unscrupulous fertility clinic operators, traffickers in clonal embryos, and out-and-out racist eugenicists.

Today, in 2021, the genetic scientists and their political and military commanders have lost any sense of identification with the larger human community. In their minds the well-being of any existing human cannot be allowed to stand in the way of the historical transition to a post-human future. But they differ about who will supply the foundational human stock.

And if it seems that things could not get any worse, just last week a doomsday cult announced that it has perfected and is about to release the "Elysium Virus," a genetically engineered hyper-viroid that inactivates neural calcium ion channels. Its release would rapidly destroy all life on Earth above the level of a sponge. The cult has issued no demands; its members say they are driven by an altruistic desire to relieve "all sentient beings" of the burden of existence. The world is holding its breath, teetering on the verge of panic.

Scenario Four: For the Common Good

The opening years of the 21st century were marked by controversy over cloning, stem cells, and human genetic modification. Opinion surveys showed strong support for the development of genetic technology for medical purposes, but controversies involving blackmail attempts using stolen sperm donor records, the deaths of clonal primates at a lab in Oregon, and shady financial practices by leading bioethicists began to raise doubts. Although the new genetic technologies attracted many sincere, socially responsible researchers, by 2009 the field was increasingly dominated by dismissively arrogant scientists, unscrupulous fertility clinic operators, traffickers in clonal embryos, and out-and-out racist eugenicists.

Reaction from the general public and affected constituencies had been building for some time, and by 2010 reached a tipping point. Advocates for women's health, consumer rights, and economic justice raised concerns about risky technologies that put corporate profits above safe, affordable health care. Civil rights leaders warned of a new free market eugenics that could stoke the fires of racial and ethnic hatred. Disability rights leaders charged that a society obsessed with genetic perfection could come to regard the disabled as mistakes that should have been prevented. Civil libertarians were appalled to learn of plans by global biotech consortia to establish a universal DNA registry. Lesbians and gays were disturbed by reports that prenatal tests for sexual orientation were about to be made commercially available. Environmentalists argued that genetic modification of living organizations including humans was a powerfully disruptive technology being deployed before long-range consequences had been considered.

In 2011 liberal and conservative religious denominations put aside their doctrinal differences and convened an international summit that declared the genetic modification of the human species to be a threat to human dignity and the human community. Later that year the Citizens Health Assembly, representing hundreds of international health, development, and indigenous rights organizations, began a major campaign opposing the global biotechnology industry's drive to have human genomics declared the lead technology for addressing public health problems in poor countries.

The first credible reports of covert attempts to create clonal and genetically modified children appeared in early 2012. The efforts were taking place on a fleet of converted naval hospital ships sailing the South Pacific and guarded by gunboats. The identities of the scientists involved were unclear. Responsible political and scientific leaders realized that a strong response was in order. In late 2012 a group of internationally recognized scientists and health policy experts declared that the new human biotechnologies "carry with them both great promise and great risk," and that scientists must be willing to work within socially determined limits. The declaration received extensive press coverage and commentary.

A Common Framework

In 2013 a bipartisan group of U.S. senators began meeting to broker a broadly acceptable, comprehensive package of human biotech regulations. All involved agreed to take the issues of abortion and the moral status of human embryos off the table, and to focus on policies on which it appeared that consensus might be reached. As it turned out, this was easier than had been anticipated. Embryonic stem cell research was allowed but "designer baby" applications and human cloning were banned, and a new federal commission was established to oversee human biotech research. In 2015 the final bill was signed into law.

The following year, international civil society leaders prevailed upon the United Nations to convene the Extraordinary Summit on Bioscience and the Human Future. Delegates included noted scientists, political leaders, scholars, and representatives of the full spectrum of social and religious constituencies. Negotiations were contentious and frequently threatened to break down. But the delegates realized that this might be the last chance humanity would have to agree upon a common framework for regulating these powerful technologies, and by 2018 success was in sight. In 2019 the UN General Assembly approved the Universal Convention on Biomedicine and Human Rights by a nearly unanimous vote. In 2020 the convention went into force after having been approved by the parliaments of 110 countries. All involved recognized that they had participated in an undertaking of world-historical import. Just last month, the 2021 Nobel Prizes for Medicine and Peace were jointly awarded to the lead institutions that had made this all possible: the United Nations, the World Assembly of Science, the Global Council of Religions, and the NGO Network for a Human Future. . . .

We need to think of the issues before us and the frameworks through which we interpret them in new ways.

Effective International Control

"For the Common Good" incorporates many of my own values and hopes, and is presented as a more-or-less straightforward success story. But the road to any agreements of the sort sketched here will surely be filled with bumps and detours. Conflicts over the new human biotechnologies, like most other conflicts, involve the eternal tension between competition and cooperation among individuals, families, communities, and nations. New technologies developed over the past century have enabled individuals and groups to compete in ways that could endanger humanity as a whole. It's widely acknowledged that humanity needs to develop shared values and institutions that will allow such universal threats to be avoided. Attempts to do this, from the United Nations to bans on nuclear weapons to the Kyoto Accords, have had mixed success.

The noted writer Bill McKibben once said, correctly, that the greatest macroscale environmental challenge is global warming and the greatest microscale environmental challenge is genetic engineering. Technologies that enable humanity to manipulate individual atoms, molecules, genes, and cells are being used to radically transform the fundamental processes of the natural world including many of those that define what it means to be human.

It is imperative that individuals and organizations committed to a sustainable, just, and truly human future take steps to bring these technologies under effective national and international oversight and control. To do this we need to think of the issues before us and the frameworks through which we interpret them in new ways. There is no greater challenge, and time is short.

Genetic Technology Poses Risks and Needs International Regulation

Brad Sherman

Brad Sherman has been a Democratic member of the United States House of Representatives since 1997, representing California's Twenty-seventh Congressional District.

Advances in the field of human genetics have the potential to provide humanity with invaluable benefits—namely, the ability to identify, diagnose, treat and prevent some of the world's worst maladies in ways that were unthinkable less than a few decades ago. But these technologies also raise some of the most complex moral issues ever to confront humanity; they have the potential to impact our society in fundamental ways; indeed they raise existential questions for humanity.

When, if ever, should it be permissible to utilize genetic technology, not to alleviate someone's suffering, but to actually enhance a normal human being? How will we draw the line between "therapies" and "enhancements"?

The Impact of Science

I believe that the impact of science on this century will be far greater than the enormous impact science had on the last century. As futurist Christine Peterson notes: If someone is describing the future 30 years from now and they paint a picture that seems like it is from a science fiction movie, then they might be wrong. But, if someone is describing the future a generation from now and they paint a picture that doesn't

Brad Sherman, "Committee on Foreign Affairs, Subcommittee on Terrorism, Nonproliferation, and Trade, Hearing on Genetics and other Human Modification Technologies: Sensible International Regulation or a New Kind of Arms Race? (Prepared Statement)," House of Representatives: Committee on Foreign Affairs, Subcommittee on Terrorism, Nonproliferation, and Trade, June 19, 2008, pp. 3–5.

look like a science fiction movie, then you know they are wrong. . . . We are going to live in a science fiction movie, we just don't know which one.

There is one issue that I think is more explosive than even the spread of nuclear weapons: engineered intelligence. By "engineered intelligence" I mean the efforts of computer engineers and bioengineers to create intelligence beyond that of a human being. As we develop more intelligent computers, we will find them useful tools in creating evermore intelligent computers, a positive feedback loop.

The undeniable benefits of the computer and DNA research are arriving long before the problematic possibilities.

The history of nuclear technology is analogous to the potential rapid development of advanced technologies for human modification. On August 2, 1939, [physicist Albert] Einstein sent [President Franklin D.] Roosevelt a letter saying a nuclear weapon was possible; six years later, nuclear technology literally exploded onto the world scene. Only after society saw the negative effects of nuclear technology, did we see the prospects for nuclear power and nuclear medicine.

The future of engineered intelligence will be different. The undeniable benefits of the computer and DNA research are arriving long before the problematic possibilities. Their introduction will be gradual, not explosive. And fortunately, we will have far more than six years to consider the implications—unless we choose to squander the next few decades. My fear is that our philosophers, ethicists and society at large, will ignore the issues that will inevitably present themselves until . . . they actually present themselves. And these issues require more than a few years of thought.

Morally Questionable Activity

The easiest and cheapest thing that can be done with this topic is to say that we shouldn't talk about it because it is subject to mockery. If people disagree with these points let them argue seriously and not substitute cheap derision for serious discussion. I could argue that some of the types of technology that I have just referred to will be actually feasible this century if scientists are inclined to achieve that result. Some will argue that Western scientists will not do the kinds of morally questionable activity necessary to develop some of these technologies.

First, remember that North Korea developed a nuclear bomb, albeit long after the West. And if you think North Korea will be constrained by morality or our conception of human rights when proceeding with its scientific research, reflect that this is a government that kidnapped nearly 500 civilians from other countries and starved hundreds of thousands of its own citizens—will they be reluctant to manipulate an embryo?

In the absence of international consensus binding all nations, some states will attempt to manipulate human genetics and other technologies to gain some advantage.

Second, some of what we are talking about today can be accomplished using animal rather than human DNA. Are all Western scientists adverse to playing with dolphin embryos or concerned that a dolphin with enhanced intelligence might pose a moral dilemma? I don't think so.

Third, many of these technologies will get safer as decades go by, and the benefits in treating disease will be more and more enticing.

Fourth, one of the potential technologies related to our topic today, implanting computer chips in humans, may pose less risks to a human subject than genetic engineering.

Again, we cannot assume that others around the world will reach the same conclusions we do. Rather, we need to approach this issue assuming quite the opposite: In the absence of international consensus binding all nations, some states will attempt to manipulate human genetics and other technologies to gain some advantage, perhaps even a military advantage.

Military Use of Genetic Research

If we do not develop some international consensus on controlling this technology, and if we fail to enforce any consensus that does emerge, we can anticipate a world where rogue (and even not-so-rogue) states and non-state actors attempt to manipulate human genetics in ways that will horrify us.

Those who say mankind will never manipulate the genome for military purposes must count themselves with those who would have said that mankind would never manipulate the atom for military purposes. Or that mankind would limit itself to just enough nuclear weapons to win World War II, but not enough to endanger the entire planet.

In fact, we are already working to enhance humans for military uses. Currently, the Defense Advanced Research Projects Agency (DARPA), the Department of Defense's research arm, is pouring millions into a "Peak Soldier Performance" program aimed at creating technologies to improve a soldier's performance in combat. DARPA would like to create a soldier that eats and sleeps less without any significant long-term consequences. Will these same technologies be available to students taking their SATs [Scholastic Assessment Tests]?

We are not doomed to the dangerous and the immoral. But if we refuse to think of the diplomatic and ethical issues that confront us this century because we are sublimely confident in the goodness and morality of all human actors, then we will be a bit naïve.

Mockery of those who wish to exam[ine] the issues that will confront us, or Pollyannaish belief that these issues will somehow be swept away, is just as wrong as a Luddite [person opposed to technological change] that would cause us to halt all genetic research in its tracks. We should neither bow to the ethical problems that we will confront nor ignore them.

A Treaty Such as the Nuclear Non-Proliferation Treaty

One of our witnesses today [June 19, 2008, during a congressional hearing] has put forward the idea of a treaty to help define the permissible uses of technology, specifically using the model of the Nuclear Non-Proliferation Treaty (the NPT). Why the NPT and why the underlying comparison to nuclear technology?

It is clear that we should develop some internationally agreed standards to prevent the misuse of these technologies.

First, the NPT assumes that countries will want to utilize nuclear power for legitimate purposes and provides a guarantee that they will have access to it. In return for forgoing the right to develop nuclear weapons, countries will receive access to civilian nuclear technology. As with nuclear power—indeed even more so—people from all countries should enjoy the benefits of the "legitimate" uses of genetic technology, whatever we determine those to be. As we look to potential regulation, whether international or domestic, we should be concerned with ensuring the widest possible access to the beneficial uses of genetic technologies.

Second, the legitimate uses of the technologies provide the means, and may provide the cover, for a nefarious program. You can operate a nuclear reactor for the generation of electricity or for the production of weapons-grade plutonium. The same may be true of genetic and other technologies—the knowledge and infrastructure you acquire in seemingly legitimate pursuits may be put to use for nefarious purposes. Likewise, as with nuclear power—the operation of what looks like a legitimate program of research may serve as "cover" for a program that is illegitimate.

Whether or not a treaty modeled on the NPT is the best approach, it is clear that we should develop some internationally agreed standards to prevent the misuse of these technologies. Of course, there is no IAEA [International Atomic Energy Agency] for genetics and related technologies, so enforcement mechanisms will have to be developed, and that will be a major challenge. But it is imperative that we try.

The last time a new, higher level of intelligence arose on this planet was roughly 50,000 years ago. It was our own ancestors, who then said hello to the previously most intelligent species, the Neanderthals. It did not work out so well for the Neanderthals.

Genetic Technology Will Impact Mental Health in Addition to Physical Health

Arthur L. Caplan

Arthur L. Caplan is Emanuel and Robert Hart Professor of Bioethics and director of the Center for Bioethics at the University of Pennsylvania School of Medicine.

For too long, mental health has been a policy and ethical backwater. While mountains of articles have been written on the ethics of cloning human beings (hugely unlikely to happen anytime soon), the morality of using genetically engineered animals as sources of organs for transplants (ditto), and the moral defensibility of using treatments derived from embryonic stem cell research to cure horrific diseases (a very long shot), hardly any literature exists on the ethics of current practices and policies in mental health.

A Revolution in Mental Health

All that is about to change. A technological revolution imminent in mental health will soon revolutionize how mental illness is widely perceived and elevate it to the forefront of health policy.

Mental illnesses will surely be the newest targets for genetic testing.

We have all heard, perhaps to the point of indifference, about the mapping of the human genome. With dramatic technological advances, we have jumped from having a rudimentary chromosomal map of our genes and those of other animals and plants to a finely tuned, high resolution blueprint of human DNA. Think of the transformation from a basic map of the world's continents and oceans to the ability to locate your own front yard through satellite imagery on Google Earth, and you'll begin to understand the enormity.

Most of the discussion about the benefits of mapping the human genome has focused on diagnosing physical disorders or the risk of acquiring them. Breast cancer, heart disease, deafness, cystic fibrosis, Fanconi's anemia, hemophilia, and similar maladies have been the poster children in the emerging era of precision genetic testing. But, as genomic knowledge expands and as more databases involving all aspects of the health of millions of people are correlated with an ever-increasing number of genes, mental illnesses will surely be the newest targets for genetic testing. This means that embryos, fetuses, children, and adults will soon be candidates for testing for a vast range of risks and predispositions: addiction, depression, anxiety, schizophrenia, phobias, paranoia, obsessive-compulsive disease, aggressive behavior, attention deficit disorders, and many other mental impairments. Doctors will soon be able to detect the risk of developing mental illnesses as accurately as they now detect many physical illnesses.

New Controversies

The expansion of genomics into mental health will bring much good in the form of prevention and early diagnosis. It will also bring much controversy. Among the many thorny questions to be answered: Should genetic testing for risks of developing mental diseases be entirely voluntary? How private should such tests be? How much counseling ought to accompany the tests, and who should do the counseling? How accurate must these tests be before being made available to doctors, employers, or to the public directly in home-test kits?

And, critically, what exactly constitutes a "mental illness" for which testing would be worthwhile in the first place?

This is not the stuff of science fiction. At least one company, San Diego-based Psynomics, is offering a home-test kit for a gene associated with bipolar disease and depression. A buyer spits in a cup and sends the sample off to Psynomics for testing. It is not at all clear that the test is accurate enough to justify its widespread use. Nor are doctors ready to explain the results of the test to those who buy these kits. Nor is it clear how to protect someone from having their saliva taken and sent off without their permission—say by someone who swabs your mouth while you sleep or takes some of your DNA off a coffee cup or glass.

Neuroimaging Technology

Right along with the explosion in knowledge about the genetic contribution to mental illness is another new and powerful, if less attention-grabbing, technology—neuroimaging. We have all seen the fascinating pictures of how our brains "light up" in response to certain stimuli or thought patterns. Scanning technologies far more powerful than the familiar CAT scan—tests like positron emission tomography, functional magnetic resonance imaging, multichannel electroencephalography, and near infrared spectroscopic imaging—already make it possible to "watch" neural activity in real time with impressive accuracy. Since the link between the brain and your behavior is a lot closer than it is between your genes and your behavior, imaging the brain through these and other technological advances is likely to prove to be the biggest boon ever to the mental health field.

Long before symptoms actually appear, a brain scan may reveal early onset Alzheimer's [disease], antisocial tendencies, or autism; show patterns predictive of depression or suicidal ideation later in life; or prove predictive of who will find themselves getting into trouble in junior high school. Conditions that are now difficult to diagnose, such as mild schizo-phrenia or Asperger's [disorder], may prove easily detected when imaging results confirm suspicions.

Where is neuroimaging taking us? Want to claim that you need extra time on an exam due to a learning disability? You may need to undergo a neuroimaging exam to confirm your diagnosis. Hope to convince a parole board that you are ready to be discharged from prison after having undergone extensive therapy for child molestation? An intensive brain examination taken while you are exposed to suggestive photos may prove your case and secure a release sooner than a therapist's diagnosis will. And before anyone prescribes an antidepressant to a very young person, both a neuroimaging study and genetic testing may be required to assess the child's risk profile for dangerous, adverse events and unwanted side effects that the drug might cause.

The range and complexity of ethical issues raised by neuroimaging are as impressive as any that have accompanied any recent technological development in health care.

It is not just medicine that will be responding to the explosion of diagnostic power that will flow from advances in genomics and neuroimaging. The ability to detect an abnormal brain may begin to shift thinking in the courts and criminal justice system away from a punishment perspective toward a more therapeutic or medical model. If you are facing the death sentence in a highly controversial case, how quickly can your lawyer introduce a picture of your brain that shows gross abnormalities inconsistent with personal responsibility? Similarly, mental health workers may find themselves called upon more and more often to offer their prognoses about who is likely to steal, embezzle, or harass at work. Before long, neuroimaging exams may supplant many of the familiar psychological and aptitude tests used in schools and the workplace today. And how long will it be before exclusive private nursery schools and kindergartens add a request for a brain-scan analysis to their admissions requirements?

The range and complexity of ethical issues raised by neuroimaging are as impressive as any that have accompanied any recent technological development in health care. Who will be paying for all this testing? When will such testing be mandatory—upon entry to the military or the clergy, upon arrest, when seeking a marriage license? Who will do the testing, who will be able to see the results, and what standards will they answer to?

The Future of Mental Health

The technology rolling toward us will even change how we think about mental health and mental illness. Today, drug abusers stick themselves with needles, risking diseases and addiction to get high. Tomorrow, you may be able to feed a signal right into the pleasure centers of your brain, giving you a much greater high without all the mess and risk. Is that a good thing? What if someone chooses to stay in a virtual world, remain attached to a pleasure-stimulating machine, or try to use new drugs or devices to boost their performance, mood, or sex drive or even modify a personality trait they don't like? Is "cosmetic" mental health a field of which our children will partake? Will debates about what to do about mental illness expand far beyond those we currently recognize as mentally ill?

What can be used to treat can also be used to enhance.

There is also, of course, a profoundly positive side to this story. Improvements in diagnostics will guarantee improvements in treatments for millions of people suffering brain-related disorders. Already, better neuroimaging permits doctors to implant devices aimed at treating parkinsonism or epilepsy deep into the brain. More precision forms of psycho-surgery and a wider range of implantable gizmos are very likely to follow.

Similarly, advances in our ability to "pinpoint" drugs to an individual patient's genetic or neural makeup will bring enormous benefits. Today, we must often rely on "one-size-fits-all" drugs that can be associated with serious risks and side effects. Tomorrow, when treatments become more and more efficacious with fewer and fewer problems, issues of access to care and the moral imperative to pay for it will come center stage in health policy debates.

The New Technology

What can be used to treat can also be used to enhance. So the nascent trend in high schools and colleges among students and faculty to try drugs that help focus attention, or to permit a person to stay awake and function with less sleep, is likely to evolve into an enormous societal debate about the use of drugs or implants to boost productivity. Our grandchildren may well find that certain career paths are not open to them unless they are willing to undergo psychosurgery or take powerful cognition-enhancing drugs.

If the technology is built, then the field of mental health will bear little resemblance to the struggling, underfunded, often stigmatized, and somewhat mundane set of activities grouped under the mental health banner that we are familiar with today. Mental health is about to fulfill the old Freudian dream—resting psychiatry and psychology on a neuroscientific and biological foundation. That may not guarantee the delivery of the best mental health care to those in need, but it will guarantee a revolution in the attitudes, expectations, and utilization of mental health care services and knowledge. What once was a field fighting for parity and battling stigma is on the cusp of becoming a field where you would have to be crazy not to at least consider using what mental health will have to offer.

CHAPTER 2

What Are Some Concerns About Genetic Testing?

Overview: Concerns About Genetic Testing

Genetics & Public Policy Center

The Genetics & Public Policy Center was created in 2002 at Johns Hopkins University to help policy makers, the press, and the public understand and respond to the challenges and opportunities of genetic medicine.

Genetic testing has grown dramatically in the past decade, and increasingly is becoming an integral part of health care. Currently, genetic tests for more than 1,000 different diseases are available clinically, and several hundred more are under development. These tests can help diagnose genetic conditions and guide treatment decisions, help predict risk of future disease, inform reproductive decision making, and assist medication choices or dosing.

The growing use of genetic testing raises a number of questions about how an individual's genetic information can be used. In particular, can employers use genetic information to make hiring and firing decisions? Can insurance companies deny people coverage based on their genetic test results?

Fear of Genetic Discrimination

Despite widespread, long-standing agreement among American citizens and politicians that protection from genetic discrimination should be clear and consistent, at this time (2007) an individual's genetic information is protected only by a largely untested patchwork of state and federal regulations. Many states have enacted protections against genetic discrimi-

"U.S. Public Opinion on Uses of Genetic Information and Genetic Discrimination," Genetics & Public Policy Center, April 24, 2007. www.dnapolicy.org. Reproduced by permission.

nation in health insurance, employment, or both. However, these state laws vary widely in scope and many are untested in court. State laws fail to provide a uniform floor of protections in employment and health insurance on which Americans can rely.

Meanwhile, individual patients who could benefit from genetic testing are in some cases foregoing it out of concern over possible repercussions. A 2004 study of 470 people with a family history of colorectal cancer showed that nearly half rated their level of concern about genetic discrimination as high. Those individuals with high levels of concern indicated that they would be significantly less likely to consider even meeting with a health care professional to discuss genetic testing, or to undergo testing. When people opt not to be tested, they lose the opportunity to seek monitoring and preventive care to forestall or avoid conditions for which they are at higher risk. This fear of genetic discrimination negatively affects not only patients, but also health insurers (who will pay more to treat conditions that are not caught early) and employers (when employees require more sick days and medical leave).

Enthusiasm about genetic testing is tempered by widespread public concern and distrust about the discrimination that could result.

Moreover, the threat of discrimination hinders both genetic research and clinical practice. Linking gene variants to health outcomes often requires studies involving large numbers of people, but scientists report that many potential subjects are deterred by the fear that their information could be used against them by employers or insurers. Thus, research is impeded that would help to bring about the much-heralded era of personalized medicine.

Views Regarding Genetic Testing

In 2007 the Genetics & Public Policy Center surveyed 1,199 Americans over the age of 18 to measure public acceptance of the use of genetic testing for medical and nonmedical purposes, to examine whom they do and do not trust with their genetic information, and gauge their support or lack thereof for laws that would protect them from some forms of genetic discrimination. . . .

Among the principal findings:

- The majority of Americans enthusiastically support genetic testing for research and health care, but a large majority (92%) also express concern that results of a genetic test that tells a patient whether he or she is at increased risk for a disease like cancer could be used in ways that are harmful to the person.

- Majorities also said that they would trust doctors and genetic researchers to have access to genetic test results. However, only one person in four would trust health insurers, and 16% would trust employers, to have access to his or her genetic test results.

- Nearly all Americans believe that health insurers and employers should not be able to deny or limit insurance coverage or to make decisions about hiring and promotion based on genetic test results about their risk of future disease. Three of every four Americans support a law forbidding genetic discrimination by health insurers and employers.

- Support for laws prohibiting employment and health insurance genetic discrimination was consistently strong among different groups of Americans—at least 68% of all genders, racial/ethnic groups, ages, and levels of education and household income supported laws against both types of discrimination. Support for both laws increased with education and household income.

Tempered Enthusiasm

Americans clearly support the use of genetic testing to further their own health and the health of their families. The public also supports the use of genetic testing in medical research. However, this enthusiasm about genetic testing is tempered by widespread public concern and distrust about the discrimination that could result if insurers and employers access and use genetic test results.

Legislative Protection from Genetic Discrimination Is Necessary

Louise Slaughter

Louise Slaughter has been a Democratic member of the U.S. House of Representatives since 1987, representing New York's Twenty-eighth Congressional District.

I am the only member of Congress that has a masters in public health and I am a microbiologist by training and health care policy has been a special interest of mine since I first came to Congress 22 years ago. I have always strived to ensure that our nation's health policies are grounded in accurate science.

I'm here today to talk about the Genetic Information Nondiscrimination Act, or GINA for short. I worked on this landmark law for 13 years. . . .

Genetic Tests for Disease

As most of you know, in 1991, Congress initiated the Human Genome Project as a collaborative effort with the Department of Health and Human Services and the Department of Energy with the purpose of decoding the human genetic sequence.

Three years later, the field of medicine was transformed by the discovery of the first genetic mutation linked to breast cancer.

Then in 2003, researchers completed the sequencing of the human genome. This momentous event threw open the doors of opportunity and researchers have been able to identify genetic markers for a number of chronic health conditions.

Louise Slaughter, "The Genetic Information Nondiscrimination Act: A New Way for Health Care: Rep. Slaughter's Remarks to the Harvard Graduate School of Arts and Sciences Science Policy Group and the Biomedical Graduate Student Organization," U.S. House of Representatives Louise Slaughter's Web site: www.louise.house.gov, April 17, 2009.

A thorough understanding of genetics offers great potential for early treatment and the prevention of numerous diseases.

Just because a person tests positive for a genetic mutation, there should be no assumptions that the person will develop that disease.

As more genetic links to diseases have been identified, genetic tests have become commercially available, and genetic technology has become firmly embedded in the practice of medicine.

Everything from cancer to heart disease and diabetes are known to have a genetic component.

It is estimated that all humans are genetically predisposed to between five and 50 serious disorders. None of us ... has perfect genes.

It is important to note that just because a person tests positive for a genetic mutation, there should be no assumptions that the person will develop that disease. Genetic tests that reveal genetic mutations simply indicate risk. Despite testing positive for a genetic mutation, an individual may remain asymptomatic over his entire lifetime.

However, the ability to decode which diseases we are predisposed to, or at risk for, leaves each of us vulnerable to discrimination.

There were some in Congress who called GINA "a solution in search of a problem" and suggested that genetic discrimination is rare, if it happened at all.

Unfortunately, genetic discrimination was happening and it was well documented.

Examples of Genetic Discrimination

In 2004, Congress and the Secretary's Advisory Committee on Genetics, Health, and Society heard from several victims of such discrimination.

Prominent examples also include a 2000 case where the Burlington Northern Santa Fe Railway performed genetic tests on employees without their knowledge or consent. The workers involved had applied for workers' compensation, and the tests were conducted to undermine their claims. One such worker had refused to submit a blood sample for genetic testing, and consequently was threatened with termination. Burlington Northern Santa Fe Railway settled these cases in April 2001 for $2.2 million.

A few years earlier in 1998, Lawrence Berkeley National Laboratory was found to have been performing tests for syphilis, pregnancy, and sickle-cell anemia on employees without their knowledge or consent for years. Throughout the 1970s, many African Americans were denied jobs, educational opportunities, and insurance based on their carrier status for sickle-cell anemia, again, despite the fact that a carrier lacked the two copies of a mutation necessary to get sick.

We also heard from:

- A North Carolinian woman who when her genetic tests revealed a risk for a lung disorder was fired even though she had begun the treatments that would keep her healthy;

- A social worker whom, despite outstanding performance reviews, was fired because of her employer's fears about her family history of Huntington's disease;

- An adoption agency refusing to allow a woman at risk for Huntington's disease to adopt a child; and

- A woman who was tested and diagnosed with alpha-1 antitrypsin deficiency, which she could control with medication. Shortly following her diagnosis, she lost her job. Without employment, and having a pre-existing condition, she also lost her health, life and disability insurance.

A 1996 study showed that a number of institutions including health and life insurance companies, health care providers, adoption agencies, the military, and schools were reported to have engaged in genetic discrimination against asymptomatic individuals.

Given the prevalence of genetic discrimination, many individuals are deciding against having genetic tests or participating in genetic research.

A 2001 American Management Association survey of employer medical testing practices found that 1.3 percent of companies test new or current employees for sickle-cell anemia, 0.4 percent test for Huntington's disease, and 20.1 percent ask about family medical history. When asked if the results were used in hiring, reassigning, retaining or dismissing employees, 1 percent of employers indicated that sickle cell, 0.8 percent indicated that Huntington's, and 5.5 percent indicated that family history results were used.

Fear of Genetic Discrimination

Given the prevalence of genetic discrimination, many individuals are deciding against having genetic tests or participating in genetic research.

Others are opting to take genetic tests under an assumed name or pay out-of-pocket in order to learn valuable information about their potential future health status, but not have it used against them.

In a 2006 Cogent Research poll, 66 percent of respondents said they had concerns about how their genetic information would be stored and who would have access. Sixty-five percent said they were concerned about health insurance companies, and 54 percent were concerned with employers gaining unauthorized access.

Health care professionals also are hesitant to make genetic information available. In one survey of genetic counselors, 108 out of 159 indicated that they would not submit charges for a genetic test to their insurance companies primarily because of the fear of discrimination. Twenty-five percent responded that they would use an alias to obtain a genetic test in order to reduce the risk of discrimination and maximize confidentiality. Moreover, 60 percent indicated that they would not share the information with a colleague, because of the need for privacy and fear of job discrimination.

Studies also have shown that even if early detection of a particular genetic mutation may help avert premature morbidity and mortality, Americans are still deciding to forego genetic testing altogether due to fears of discrimination.

GINA . . . will provide critical protections against genetic discrimination for all Americans.

Hereditary nonpolyposis colorectal cancer (HNPCC) provides an instructive example. Six genes have been identified to determine if a person carries a mutation for HNPCC. HNPCC is the most common hereditary form of colon cancer and it is estimated that 380,000 Americans carry an HNPCC mutation. Those with the mutation have a 90 percent lifetime risk of developing one of the cancers associated with HNPCC. Between 1996 and 1999, people identified from families with the HNPCC mutations were asked to participate in a study that offered genetic testing for the mutation. While there were other considerations for not participating in the study, of those who declined genetic testing, 39 percent cited fears about losing health insurance as the reason.

The high fear factor led the authors of this study to conclude that without legal protections at the national level to address the public's fear of discrimination, a significant number of Americans will opt not to reap the benefits of advanced screening for cancer that would lead to healthier, longer lives.

The Genetic Information Nondiscrimination Act

We have laws to protect us from discrimination based on race, gender, and a host of other intrinsic characteristics. We desperately needed to enact similar law to protect against genetic discrimination not only to ensure that the tremendous potential of genetic testing and research could be realized but because it was the right thing to do.

GINA, now Public Law 110-233, will provide critical protections against genetic discrimination for all Americans.

Specifically, GINA will prevent health insurers from canceling, denying, refusing to renew, or changing the terms or premiums of coverage based on genetic information.

It also will prohibit employers from making hiring, firing, promotion, and other employment-related decisions based on genetic factors.

Because more than 61.8 percent of Americans get their insurance through their employers, without job security, there are no guarantees of insurance protections. If [individuals] are protected from insurers but not their employers, they could be fired and lose their insurance coverage anyway. That is why it was critical for GINA to prohibit discrimination by both health insurers and employers.

Title I applies to employer-sponsored group health plans, health insurance issuers in the group and individual markets, Medigap insurance, and state and local nonfederal governmental plans.

Title II extends prohibitions to employers, unions, employment agencies, and labor-management training programs.

As I mentioned, I first introduced genetic antidiscrimination legislation in 1995. Just last year, in 2008, GINA became law. . . .

GINA states that Title I takes effect in May 2009 and Title II takes effect in November 2009.

This was done to allow the federal government to provide regulatory guidance as to how to implement the law. We have just completed this stage now.

The departments of Treasury, Health and Human Services, and Labor and the Equal Employment Opportunity Commission are in the process or have already completed regulations for GINA.

The potential for genetic medicine is limitless.

The Pace of Genetic Research

Meanwhile, genetic research is progressing at a rapid pace.

Researchers have identified genetic markers for a variety of chronic health conditions and increased the potential for early treatment and the prevention of numerous genetic-based diseases. There are already genetic tests for over 1,000 diseases, and hundreds more are under development.

The potential for genetic medicine is limitless. For example, it was about a year ago that the researchers at Moorefields Eye Hospital in London announced they had restored some eyesight to people who were disposed to a genetic disease that harmed their vision as children. To be able to restore eyesight is something none of us had ever dreamed of being able to do. But by injecting genetic material into the back of the eye behind the retina, they have received some sight. Researchers believe that once they are able to do this in younger children and are able to increase the dose that the success rate will be extremely high, and that, in itself, is such good news.

With workplace and health insurance protections in place, I believe we can dramatically change the way we do health care in this country. People will be more inclined to obtain genetic testing and may be able to prevent or at least seek out early treatment for a number of diseases, thereby cutting down on long hospital stays and costly end-of-life treatments.

The Demand for Genetic Testing

Some of you may have heard about my colleague, Congresswoman Debbie Wasserman Schultz. She represents Pembroke Pines, Florida, and she's only 43 years old.

A few weeks ago, she bravely went public about her year-long battle with breast cancer. During that time, she would fly to Washington, D.C., for votes and then fly back to Florida for treatments.

They will be more inclined to seek out early testing for genetic predispositions without fear of job or health insurance discrimination.

In speaking about her ordeal, Congresswoman Wasserman Schultz has discussed the fact that as a woman of Ashkenazi Jewish descent, she was in a category of at-risk populations for the BRCA1 and BRCA2 gene mutation. Because of her family history, after she was diagnosed with breast cancer, she decided to get the genetic test and found out that she carried the BRCA2 genetic marker that suggests a greater susceptibility to breast and ovarian cancers. She also underwent a double mastectomy.

At no point during the year did we have any idea that she was ill.

She is now dedicated to educating young Ashkenazi Jewish women about the need for early and frequent breast cancer screenings and is encouraging them to get the genetic test for the BRCA1 and BRCA2 genes.

Whereas just a couple years ago, doctors cautioned women against overtly seeking a genetic test.

Now I can wholeheartedly support her efforts and am so proud that GINA will convey protections to at-risk groups like

Ashkenazi Jewish women and hopefully they will be more inclined to seek out early testing for genetic predispositions without fear of job or health insurance discrimination.

When GINA is implemented this year [2009], I believe many more Americans will participate in genetic testing and the demand for genetic tests will grow.

Legislative Protection from Genetic Discrimination May Harm People

Ani B. Satz

Ani B. Satz is associate professor at the Emory University School of Law and Rollins School of Public Health.

On Wednesday [May 21, 2008], President [George W.] Bush signed the Genetic Information Nondiscrimination Act [GINA], affording genetic information special protections. A product of more than a decade of debate, this moment was bittersweet. GINA may harm many of the individuals it is designed to protect.

Concerns About GINA

The act increases protections only for some medical information, privileging those with genetic conditions over those with nongenetic ones. This necessarily places greater pressure on insurers to use nongenetic medical information to segregate risk. Further, it creates unequal disability protections. GINA protects individuals with genetic conditions from health insurance and employment discrimination even if they have no symptoms of the condition. The Americans with Disabilities Act protects only individuals with symptoms in regard to employment, services and public accommodation.

GINA also creates the perception that genetic testing is unique and not basic health care. This may further limit already restricted coverage of such technologies under public and private health insurance. In addition, heightened protections for genetic testing may discourage insurers from cover-

Ani B. Satz, "A Not-So-Protective Law: Genetic Screening Safeguard Creates Unforeseen Inequalities, Difficulties," *Atlanta Journal-Constitution*, May 27, 2008. Reproduced by permission of the author.

ing such services out of fear that they will open themselves to increased risk of litigation for breaching patient privacy. Further, insurers and employers are likely to lose incentive to provide genetic testing when they are not allowed access to the results, as they are for other diagnostic tests.

Well-intentioned members of Congress were wrongly persuaded that genetic information is a unique form of medical information.

An Outmoded View of Genetic Information

Well-intentioned members of Congress were wrongly persuaded that genetic information is a unique form of medical information. Insurers must discriminate in differentiating between risks in order to function as insurers. Whether it is unjust to deny anyone entitlement to basic health care based on randomly chosen risk criteria—genetic or nongenetic—is a separate question from whether insurers should be able to use only nongenetic information for actuarial purposes.

The fact that genetic information is both shared (other family members might also have the same condition) and predictive of a future illness is not unique. Nongenetic tests may reveal medical information about others as well. Consider sexually transmitted disease testing of one member of a sexual partnership, tuberculosis testing within families and communities, and nongenetic cancer testing of individuals within a group exposed to environmental carcinogens.

Knowledge of exposure in these situations is also predictive.

The view that genetic information is unique—what legal scholars term "genetic essentialism"—is outmoded. This is evident when examining the statutory language of some state genetic privacy laws, which invoke strong notions of privacy originally embraced in the realm of reproductive freedom in the classic abortion case *Roe v. Wade* [1973].

These laws appear to associate genetic testing with its use in the prenatal screening and abortion context and treat genetic information as uniquely and fundamentally private.

The Reality of Applied Genetics

The reproductive model of privacy does not reflect the reality of applied genetics today, especially genetic testing. Information derived from genetic testing is no longer used almost exclusively in reproductive decisions. The ability to test for predispositions to polygenic (multigene) and multifactorial (environmentally influenced) genetic diseases brings genetic testing into the realm of routine health care delivery.

For most people, genetic testing—like cholesterol testing—is simply a tool to obtain medical information that may be beneficial to current or future health. Only a small percentage of positive genetic tests can determine future health outcomes.

The Health Insurance Portability and Accountability Act [HIPAA] is consistent with this view.

When privacy protections are increased, they should be strengthened for all patients. Increasing protections for all medical information need not mean that genetic privacy will be insufficiently protected.

Consumer Genetic Tests Need More Government Regulation

Gail H. Javitt and Kathy L. Hudson

Gail H. Javitt is a policy analyst at the Genetics & Public Policy Center and a research scientist at the Berman Institute of Bioethics at Johns Hopkins University. Kathy L. Hudson is director at the Genetics & Public Policy Center and an associate professor at the Berman Institute of Bioethics at Johns Hopkins University.

U.S. consumers generally take for granted that the government assesses the safety and effectiveness of drugs and other medical products before they are made available commercially. But for genetic tests, this generally is not the case. At the same time, the number and type of genetic tests continue to increase, and tests for more than 900 genetic diseases are now available clinically. Genetic testing is playing a growing role in health care delivery and is providing information that can be the basis for profound life decisions such as whether to undergo prophylactic mastectomy, terminate a pregnancy, or take a particular drug or dosage of a drug. Current gaps in the oversight of genetic tests, and of the laboratories that offer them, thus represent a real threat to public health.

Currently, the government exercises only limited oversight of the analytic validity of genetic tests (whether they accurately identify a particular mutation) and virtually no oversight of the clinical validity of genetic tests (whether they provide information relevant to health and disease in a patient). To the extent that oversight exists, it is distributed among several agencies, with little interagency coordination. As a result, no clear regulatory mechanism exists to guide the transition

Gail H. Javitt and Kathy Hudson, "Federal Neglect: Regulation of Genetic Testing," *Issues in Science and Technology,* vol. 22, Spring 2006, pp. 59–66, University of Texas at Dallas. Copyright © 2006 National Academy of Sciences. Reprinted by permission.

of tests from research to clinical practice, or to ensure that tests offered to patients are analytically or clinically valid. In order to protect consumers, and to help advance the potential benefits offered by genetic testing, government action is urgently needed. . . .

Several genetic tests are being advertised and sold directly to the public, both through Internet Web sites and retail stores.

Targeting Consumers

The phrase "direct to consumer" [DTC] is best known in the context of pharmaceutical advertising, where it is used to refer to advertisements that inform patients of the availability of a particular medication to treat a specific condition such as depression or erectile dysfunction, and encourage them to ask their doctor about the drug. These ads have generated controversy, with some observers arguing that the ads induce demand inappropriately and fail to inform patients adequately regarding the risks of the drugs being promoted. Nevertheless, for prescription drugs, these ads can increase demand only indirectly: The physician serves as a gatekeeper, ensuring that only those medications appropriate for a patient are prescribed. Additionally, the safety and effectiveness of the drugs have already been assessed by the FDA [U.S. Food and Drug Administration].

Direct-to-consumer (DTC) genetic testing, in contrast, encompasses three different scenarios: the advertising of a genetic test that is available only upon a health care provider's order; the advertising and sale of genetic testing directly to consumers, without the involvement of any health care provider; and the advertising and sale of testing services directly to consumers, with some involvement by a health care provider employed by the tester (for example, the laboratory). Today, several genetic tests are being advertised and sold directly to the public, both through Internet Web sites and retail stores.

Most laboratories do not currently offer genetic testing directly to the public. In fact, only about eight companies promote DTC testing through Internet Web sites for health-related conditions (excluding, for example, genetic tests such as those for paternity and ancestry). However, the growth of DTC testing is likely to continue, given the low barrier to market entry, particularly via the Internet; the rapid pace of genetic research; and the interest of consumers in self-care.

Internet-Based Testing

Tests offered over the Internet include some that are conducted routinely as part of clinical practice such as tests for mutations causing cystic fibrosis, hemochromatosis, and fragile X (an abnormality of the X chromosome leading to mental impairment and other conditions). For these types of tests, the most readily apparent differences between DTC testing and provider-based testing are who collects the sample, to whom test results are communicated, and who interprets test results. Some laboratories require a patient to provide the name of a physician and will send results only to that provider, whereas other laboratories send results directly to patients and do not request the name of a provider. Some laboratories have genetic counselors on staff to take medical and family history information and be available for questions about test results; others do not.

Internet-based DTC testing also includes another category of tests: those for conditions lacking adequate evidence of predictive value for a disease or condition in the scientific literature. Examples in these categories include "genetic profiling" to guide the selection of nutritional supplements, testing to determine propensity to depression, and testing to select an appropriate skin care regimen (also sold by the testing company). One company advertises its tests for obesity and osteoporosis susceptibility and for "oxidative stress" to the nutraceutical, personal and skin care, and weight-loss industries, which, presumably, would offer them directly to consumers.

DTC tests also now include so-called "pharmacogenetic" tests: those used to determine whether a particular medication or dosage of medication is therapeutically appropriate. Although pharmacogenetics holds the promise of improved drug efficacy and reduced adverse reactions, the endeavor is predicated on the availability of accurate and reliable genetic tests. The current lack of coherent oversight threatens to derail this promising new field. Manufacturers and laboratories can simply claim that the tests are home brews in order to avoid rigorous FDA review of their quality.

In order to avoid the harms of DTC genetic testing, some observers have proposed restricting access to tests or advertising of tests.

Avoiding Harm

The initial criticism of DTC genetic testing highlighted harms from both advertising of tests and access to tests in the absence of a health care provider intermediary. The underlying theme of these criticisms has been that consumers are vulnerable to being misled by advertisements and lack the requisite knowledge to make appropriate decisions about whether to get tested or how to interpret test results. It has been argued that consumer-directed advertisements underemphasize the uncertainty of genetic testing results, and overemphasize testing's benefits to a public that is not sophisticated enough to understand genetics. Critics argue that genetic test results are complicated because they may provide only a probability of disease occurring, and that a health care provider is needed to put the test result in context and explain its subtleties. Further, it is asserted that ads may exaggerate the risk and severity of a disease for which testing is available. Thus, DTC advertising and unmediated access will have the negative effects of increasing consumer anxiety and generating demand for unnecessary testing.

Relying on state law would probably lead to a patchwork of nonuniform requirements.

In order to avoid the harms of DTC genetic testing, some observers have proposed restricting access to tests or advertising of tests. Regulating access would involve limiting those authorized to order the tests and receive the results. Regulating advertising would involve limiting the claims that test providers could make about their tests and, potentially, limiting the media through which claims could be made.

Regulating Access

Whether health care provider authorization is required in order to obtain a genetic test, or any laboratory test, is the province of state law. Some states explicitly authorize patients to order specified laboratory tests (such as cholesterol or pregnancy tests) without a prescription from a health care provider. Other states categorically prohibit all DTC testing. And still other states are silent on the issue, meaning that individual laboratories decide whether to offer DTC testing. As of 2001, more than half of the states permitted DTC testing for at least some types of tests, whereas 18 prohibited it. Even where a provider's order is required, it may not be the case that the patient's interest is the provider's only interest; sometimes a physician employed by the laboratory is empowered to authorize testing on behalf of a patient.

Federal or state law could prohibit direct patient access to genetic tests by requiring a health care provider to order the test and receive the results. However, relying on state law would probably lead to a patchwork of nonuniform requirements; and Internet-based genetic testing, which may operate outside the reach of any one state, may make enforcement of such laws more difficult. In addition, federal or state restrictions on access would be predicated on the assumption that health care providers, unlike patients, are adequately prepared to appropriately order and interpret tests, but studies have shown that providers often have inadequate knowledge and training to provide quality genetic services.

Regulating Advertising

Federal law protects consumers against unfair, deceptive, or fraudulent trade practices including false or misleading advertising claims. Ads violate the law if they make false statements about a product or service, fail to disclose material information, or lack adequate substantiation. The Federal Trade Commission (FTC) has enforced the law against manufacturers of a variety of purported health products available without a prescription such as companies that claim that their products promote hair regrowth, cure cancer, or cause weight loss. The FTC also regulates Internet-based advertising of products including those making health claims, and the agency has conducted periodic sweeps of the Internet and sent notices warning companies of violations of the law.

To the extent that advertising is neither false nor misleading and the product or service advertised is legal, the government's ability to regulate it is highly constrained.

The FTC has asserted its jurisdiction to take action against genetic test advertising that is false or misleading, and the agency has announced a joint effort with the FDA and NIH [National Institutes of Health] to identify appropriate targets for legal action. Nevertheless, the FTC's limited resources have hampered the agency in pursuing these claims, and this limitation leads the agency to focus on claims with a high likelihood of causing serious harm to many people. Perhaps as a result of its resource shortages, the FTC appears to have taken no action against any genetic test advertisements, even those that would appear clearly false and misleading on their face.

To the extent that advertising is neither false nor misleading and the product or service advertised is legal, the government's ability to regulate it is highly constrained. The First Amendment provides broad protection for so-called "commercial speech," and the government bears a high burden of proving that speech is harmful and that restrictions are needed to mitigate or prevent such harms.

The FDA's Lack of Involvement

Some observers have proposed intervention by the FDA to limit advertising claims about genetic tests. However, the FDA's jurisdiction to regulate claims made about a product is predicated on the agency's authority to regulate the product itself. For regulated products, the FDA's authority extends to claims about these products made in their labeling (and, in the case of prescription drugs, in their advertising as well). The FDA can both mandate the disclosure of risks and warnings and prohibit claims that it believes are inadequately supported by scientific evidence.

The fact that the FDA currently does not regulate most genetic tests precludes review of claims made about those tests. The FDA's lack of involvement also can affect the FTC's response, because the FTC, in enforcing its laws against false and misleading advertising, often looks to the FDA's labeling requirements for guidance regarding appropriate claim parameters. Thus, the absence of a designated oversight body for most genetic tests also means that there is no expert agency with clear authority to assess whether advertisements appropriately disclose all pertinent information to consumers.

Laws also could be enacted to prohibit advertising of genetic testing to reduce opportunities for patients to be confused or misled or to make inappropriate decisions based on testing. Such laws, in addition to being subject to criticism as unduly paternalistic, also could be subject to challenge on First Amendment grounds to the extent that they prohibit advertising claims that are not clearly false or misleading. Furthermore, although the FTC is currently empowered to prohibit advertising claims that are clearly false and misleading, the agency is not enforcing these laws against the purveyors of any genetic tests.

Restricting access and advertising would not address fundamental concerns regarding the analytic and clinical validity of all genetic tests.

Crafting a Holistic Approach

Aside from such practical challenges, restricting access and advertising would not address fundamental concerns regarding the analytic and clinical validity of all genetic tests. Although it certainly is important that patients be adequately informed about the benefits and limitations of genetic tests, test quality is a threshold, and therefore, a more fundamental concern. Suppressing advertising about the tests would . . . limit the number of consumers who find out about the tests, and limiting direct consumer access would decrease the number of consumers who could obtain them. But neither of these potential fixes would address whether the tests are performed correctly or are supported by clinical evidence demonstrating that they correlate with current or future health status. Yet these tests can have profound consequences. A predictive genetic test—for example, one that indicates a heightened risk of hereditary breast cancer—may lead a woman to choose prophylactic mastectomy. A diagnostic genetic test—say, for prenatal diagnosis—may lead to termination of pregnancy in the absence of any corroborating medical evidence from other laboratory tests or physical examination. A pharmacogenetic test to predict drug response may lead to prescribing a particular drug at a particular dosage or, alternatively, foregoing a particular therapy.

The best approach to alleviating concerns would be a system of oversight to ensure that all genetic tests . . . are analytically and clinically valid.

Given the high stakes involved, the government needs to correct the systemic gaps in oversight that render vulnerable the quality of all genetic tests and the safety of consumers. The current system is fragmented and riddled with gaps. CLIA [Clinical Laboratory Improvement Amendments] in theory requires laboratories to demonstrate the analytic validity of all tests performed, but regulations that would better ensure analytic validity for most genetic tests have yet to be implemented. CLIA has the legislative authority to establish a genetic testing specialty, but it has chosen not to do so. The FDA has the expertise to evaluate home brew genetic tests, just as it does genetic test kits and many other diagnostic tests, but the agency lacks a clear mandate to review most genetic tests. The FDA might have the legal authority to act, but new legislation that clarifies the agency's authority would eliminate the uncertainty and give the FDA a clear mandate to act.

A System of Oversight

These hurdles could be overcome through more effective leadership at the federal level, predicated on awareness that ensuring analytic and clinical validity is essential if genetic medicine is to achieve its promise of improving health. Regulating test quality would involve establishing and enforcing standards to ensure the analytic and clinical validity of tests before they are made available to the public and to ensure that laboratories are competent to perform them and report results appropriately. Thus, the best approach to alleviating concerns would be a system of oversight to ensure that all genetic tests, whether DTC or physician-based, home brew or test kit, are analytically and clinically valid.

Although DTC testing has been a vivid and headline-grabbing development in genetics, it would be a mistake, and ultimately an unsuccessful endeavor, to focus efforts on remedying the potential harms from DTC tests without considering the entire regulatory context. Without a system in which an up-front, expert evaluation can be made with respect to the analytic and clinical validity of genetic tests, it will be difficult if not impossible to make rational decisions about who can and should order the test and receive the results and what claims are appropriate in advertising.

The time has come to shift the focus to ensuring the quality of all genetic tests. Focusing on quality would address many of the concerns raised about access and advertising and would also help to ensure the quality of all genetic tests, not just those provided directly to consumers. Although there are limits on how much the government can or should do to protect consumers, there are clear opportunities for it to provide patients and providers with greater assurance that genetic tests are accurate and reliable and to provide information that is relevant to health care decision making.

Consumer Home Genetic Tests Do Not Have Any Meaningful Application

Arthur Allen

Arthur Allen is a writer and author of the book Vaccine: The Controversial Story of Medicine's Greatest Lifesaver.

Celebrating the sequencing of the human genome five years ago, President Bill Clinton declared the decipherment of its 3 billion base pairs "the most important, most wondrous map ever produced by mankind." Enthusiasts promised that the genome project heralded an era of personalized medicine. By 2010, predicted Art Caplan, the University of Pennsylvania bioethicist, the "age of one-size-fits-all drugs" would be replaced by an era of "designer drugs" targeted to different biological groups. Soon we would all have records of our own DNA, enabling physicians and counselors to program what we ought to eat, where we should go to school, what kind of life insurance we should buy, and what antidepressants we might use.

A New Industry

In five years, the genome has indeed transformed biological research. Thanks to vast quantities of new genetic information, scientists are revealing unimagined complexity in the molecular workings of the body. Precisely because of this complexity, though, much of the data have little immediately useful meaning, and the research has produced only a trickle of medicine. The drug industry submitted 50 percent fewer applications to the Food and Drug Administration [FDA] in

2002 and 2003 than in 1997 and 1998, despite the fact that biotech research investment doubled between the two periods.

But where the angels of established medical science fear to tread, a new industry has arisen. Several companies now offer genetic scans, some available at a supermarket near you, that claim to provide all you need to "take the guesswork" out of living. So, let's get started: In the words of Sciona, a leading "nutrigenetics" company, "It's time to discover the Science of You!"

The Web site of Great Smokies [Diagnostic] Laboratory of Asheville, N.C., which sells its Genovation "profiles" through alternative practitioners, promises that "seeing the results of your Genovations test is like seeing the cards you've been dealt by nature." Sciona, a British company that recently moved to the alternative lifestyles mecca of Boulder, Colo., sells "nutrigenetics" kits, with information on heart, immune system, bone health, endocrinal, and "detoxification" genes. After sending in a cheek-swab sample of DNA, you receive a booklet describing several of your gene variations and their meanings. What can be divined from these double-helixed tea leaves? A 97-page mock-up of a model profile that Sciona showed me (cost: about $500) provided the following advice to "John Doe" based on Sciona's readouts of 34 DNA variants: Eat your vegetables, get exercise, take some vitamins, and lose a few pounds. This your mom also can tell you; Sciona co-founder Rosalynn Gill-Garrison admits as much. The difference, she says, is the magical aura surrounding genetic information, the sense of finality that comes with that knowledge—however partial and even distorted.

A Failed Promise

Some of the offerings are more tailored, though certainly not more credible. GeneLink, of Margate City, N.J., will do your "nutragenic and dermatagenic profile" and direct you to particular skin care products. Another outfit, Imagene, founded by former University of Texas pharmacologist Kenneth Blum, offers DNA testing for children with "disruptive and addictive personalities." Once the $275 test kit has confirmed that your child has "dopaminergic related Reward Deficiency Syndrome," you can buy a month's supply of pills for $60, along with a $30 oral spray that provides up to two hours of relief from unspecified "cravings."

The failed promise thus far points to the hubris of a simplified view of genetics.

As snake oil goes, these offerings are mild compared with the product that some biotech companies were putting out to investors a few years back. For a precautionary tale of genetic hype, it's hard to beat the story of Human Genome Sciences, created in the 1990s by William A. Haseltine, a Harvard AIDS researcher. Haseltine had a partnership for several years with [John] Craig Venter, an erstwhile computer brainiac at the National Institutes of Health, to begin sequencing and submitting patents on thousands of pieces of DNA. To listen to Haseltine was to believe that he had discovered a gold mine. His work, he said in 2000, "speeds up biological discovery a hundredfold, easily. Easily." He talked of finding in genes "the fountain of youth" in the form of "cellular replacement" therapies. Investors rewarded Haseltine with more than $1 billion in 2000. The drugs bombed out early in clinical trials, the stock plummeted, and Haseltine decamped with his millions to become a philanthropist. Three other big genomics companies—Incyte, Celera, and Millennium Pharmaceuticals—also failed to spin genetic discoveries into drugs.

To be fair, all four are still trying, and drug development takes time. But the failed promise thus far points to the hubris of a simplified view of genetics. Certain powerful genes cause disorders like cystic fibrosis and Tay-Sachs disease. But one-gene diseases are rare, as you may remember from high school biology; in our primitive past, most humans who carried them died before child-rearing age.

It may turn out that many inherited diseases aren't connected to genes at all.

Genes and Disease

Assiduous readers of newspaper science columns will remember the stream of announcements in the 1990s of the discovery of genes "for" everything from impulsive behavior to schizophrenia to heart disease and cancer. (Not to mention the so-called gay gene.) In the fine print, the authors of those studies made clear that they thought the genes they'd located made only small contributions to the condition in question. But even those limited effects failed to hold up in most cases. A recent literature review by Joel Hirschhorn, a geneticist at the Broad Institute in Boston, found that only six of the 166 initially reported associations of genes with a disease or trait had been replicated consistently. It may turn out that many inherited diseases aren't connected to genes at all. The genome project itself showed why this is so. Some geneticists guessed, based on the number of RNA [ribonucleic acid] transcripts discovered by the late 1990s, that there were as many as 150,000 genes in the human genome. Genomic companies like Incyte patented many of those transcripts. But the number of genes has proved to be closer to 20,000. A lot of the RNA transcripts, it turns out, play other roles in the cell that are only partially understood. Genes, per se, don't provide the whole biological, and therefore medical, story of inheritance.

New gene-hunting methods involve searching for DNA variations over the entire genome. Within a year or two, for example, scientists will have a catalog of 10 million single nucleotide polymorphisms, or SNPs, which are variations in DNA base pairs at particular stretches of the genome. The hope is that by mapping out these variations, scientists will find similar patterns in people who have predispositions to certain diseases. These variations will lead the way to more genes that make subtle contributions to disease.

The Future of Personalized Medicine

Few doubt that SNPs and other collections of biomarkers will help find some meaningful genetic links to illness. But their value for the utopian future of personalized medicine is far from clear. If genetic "errors" occur in common parts of DNA across the human species, then SNP collection will help us find those errors. But if each subgroup of humans—from Pima Indians to Mongolian shepherds to Icelanders—has a unique way, say, of becoming vulnerable to Alzheimer's [disease], then no matter how many SNPs we collect, it will be difficult to find key genetic variants that we can test for—or treat. The optimistic view is that SNPs and other data collections will locate common genes that contribute to common sources of suffering. But it will be years, if ever, before a comprehensive genetic screen could tell you how specifically to stave off a particular condition. For the foreseeable future, environmental effects will swamp the visible genetic ones. That is, no matter what your genotype is, the best health advice is to eat well and not overmuch, get exercise, and stop smoking. And in general make love, not war.

For this you should pay $500?

Newborn Genetic Screening Runs the Risk of Violating Rights

Twila Brase

Twila Brase is a public health nurse and president of the Citizens' Council on Health Care, an organization that advocates for patient and physician freedom, medical innovation, and the right of citizens to a confidential patient-doctor relationship.

Newborn screening [according to Dr. Jeffrey R. Botkin, professor of pediatrics at the University of Utah] "represents the largest single application of genetic testing in medicine." It is also [according to Dr. Nancy S. Green, medical director of the March of Dimes] "the first and largest example of systematic population-wide genetic testing." Although most states provide parents with the right to opt out of the testing program, primarily for religious reasons, only Wyoming, Maryland and Washington, D.C., require parent consent.

The Return of Eugenics

Increasingly, the specter of eugenics has emerged over state government newborn genetic screening programs. For example, *The Changing Moral Focus of Newborn Screening*, the December 2008 report issued by the President's Council on Bioethics, states:

> "Advocates of a broadened notion of 'benefit' often extol the utility of newborn screening for helping parents make future reproductive decisions. . . . But this notion of 'benefit to the family' is not unproblematic. . . . Suppose that expanded screening of an infant reveals not a fatal and incurable dis-

Twila Brase, RN, PHN, "Newborn Genetic Screening: The New Eugenics?" Citizens' Council on Health Care, April 2009. www.itsmydna.org. Reproduced by permission of Twila Brase, President of Citizens' Council on Health Care. info@cchonline.org.

ease but instead a host of genetic variants, each of which merely confers elevated risk for some condition or other. Who is to say at what point an uncovered defect becomes serious enough to warrant preventing the birth of other children who might carry it? At what point have we crossed the line from legitimate family planning to capricious and morally dubious eugenics?"

Few people discuss eugenics today. Many don't even know what the term means. Those that do probably think it could never happen again. However, former practitioners of eugenics never lost their zeal, instead seeking ways to recast eugenics in a positive light. American Eugenics Society president Frederick Osborn wrote in 1946, "Population, genetics, psychology, are the three sciences to which the eugenist must look for the factual material on which to build an acceptable philosophy of eugenics and to develop and defend practical eugenics proposals." . . .

Throughout history, proponents of eugenics have focused on the reproduction of children, either through encouraging the "healthy" to reproduce or discouraging the "unhealthy" from procreation.

Today's newborn genetic screening advocates envision a much more comprehensive program in the future.

This focus has been evidenced in history by 29 state sterilization laws, the American Eugenics Society *(1922–present)*, and the horrific Nazi campaign aimed at ridding Germany of the "unfit"—the Jews, the physically deformed, the mentally retarded, the "feebleminded," the inferior, the epileptic, the deaf, the blind, "those suffering from hereditary conditions," the deviant "asocial" and the politically dissident. That the focus on reproduction still exists today is more than troubling. . . .

Newborn Genetic Screening

Newborn screening began in 1963 with PKU testing—and unintended but devastating effects on some children. This public health genetics program was later promoted as a simple prick of a baby's heel to obtain a few drops of blood to screen not only for PKU (phenylketonuria—1 out of every 19,000 babies) but also for a few rare disorders that could benefit from early intervention. Such disorders include sickle cell disease (1 of every 1,800 babies) and argininemia (1 of every 300,000 babies).

Today's newborn genetic screening advocates envision a much more comprehensive program in the future. The Heartland Regional Genetics and Newborn Screening Collaborative looks forward to every infant being screened for at least 200 different conditions. Others predict the full genomic sequencing of each child at birth. Søren Holm writes in the book *A Companion to Genethics*:

> "Newborn screening, which is usually mandated by governments to identify and treat diseases of infancy, has been limited, for ethical reasons, to disorders where early diagnosis and treatment would benefit the newborn, but with multiplex tests the focus of testing may be expanding to include some non-treatable disorders. [Philosopher of science/author Philip] Kitcher foresees the day when parents will receive an entire 'genetic report card' at the child's birth predicting lifetime health."

Such predictive capability in the hands of government officials and others is not without significant eugenic risk. Despite scientific evidence that a single gene or a group of less than desirable genes does not condemn a person to actually getting the predicted diagnosis, those who know a person's hereditary risks may treat him or her as a threat to the health of others [according to Bruce Jennings and Elizabeth Heitman in *A Christian Response to the New Genetics*]:

"On a societal level, the goal of reducing the harmful effects of genetic disease through screening and prevention strategies may promote false analogies with the control of infectious disease and its vectors, implicitly identifying carriers of specific genetic mutations as a threat to the public health."

Others, including federal agencies, argue that the financial cost to society of debilitating genetic conditions is a matter of great concern. In 1998, the U.S. Office of Technology Assessment, in discussing the "Social and Ethical Considerations" raised by the Human Genome Project, wrote, "Human mating that proceeds without the use of genetic data about the risks of transmitting diseases will produce greater mortality and medical costs than if carriers of potentially deleterious genes are alerted to their status and encouraged to mate with no carriers or to use artificial insemination or other reproductive strategies."

Government detailing of a citizen's genome is a controversial idea, but it is not a new idea.

An Old Controversial Idea

Government detailing of a citizen's genome is a controversial idea, but it is not a new idea. In 1912, the president of the American Breeders Association—renamed the American Genetic Association in 1914—said, "Who, except the prudish, would object if public agencies gave to every person a lineage number and genetic percentage ratings, that the eugenic value of every family and of every person might be available to all who have need of the truth as to the probable efficiency of the offspring."

Perhaps a lineage number would not be sufficient to obtain the desired eugenic results. Forty years ago, Linus Pauling, a Nobel Prize winner, said the answer to stopping the spread of hereditary disorders would essentially require a tattooed "Scarlet Letter":

"I have suggested that there should be *tattooed on the forehead* of every young person a symbol showing possession of the sickle cell gene or whatever other similar gene such as the gene for phenylketonuria that has been found to possess ... If this were done, two young people carrying the same seriously defective gene ... would recognize this situation at first sight, and would refrain from falling in love with one another."

"It is my opinion that legislation along this line, compulsory testing for defective genes before marriage, and some form of semi-public display of this possession, should be adopted."

Is it thus noteworthy that the government-funded Sickle Cell Trust in Jamaica is now providing fifth and sixth grade students with the results of their sickle cell tests on a laminated card with the hope that they will "select partners with normal genes and avoid having a child with sickle cell disease." The Sickle Cell Trust has also recently set up newborn genetic screening sites to "determine whether the intervention of free screening and counseling will reduce the frequency of births with the disease." On a side note, Jamaica's oldest citizen with sickle cell disease, Isadore Simms-Franklin, turned 85 years old in 2003.

The Right to Opt Out

Although most states allow parents to refuse genetic testing—many only for religious reasons—most parents and many hospital staff are unaware of the government's involvement or the opt-out option. Parents and staff likely do not even know the testing is genetic testing.

Furthermore, the parent's right to opt out is typically only the right to refuse the testing in its entirety, not the right to choose the conditions for which their child is tested. All states screen for 21 or more conditions. California [Department of Health Care Services] screens for 76 conditions with the disclaimer that they may not actually identify an affected child:

"Due to biological variability of newborns and differences in detection rates for the various disorders in the newborn period, the Newborn Screening Program will not identify all newborns with these conditions."

To avoid giving the state health department their child's blood or genetic test results, some parents opt out of the testing altogether.

Currently, state health departments determine the list of tested conditions—some with advice from a state advisory committee. The passage of the federal Newborn Screening Saves Lives Act of 2007, enacted on April 24, 2008, will provide federal funding for the establishment of a uniform set of conditions for which all children would be tested. Today, most states have a set of mandatory tests. A few states have additional supplemental or optional tests for which parent consent is sought. Thus, testing is usually testing for all conditions—or no testing at all.

This presents a dilemma to parents who have become aware of the government's deep involvement in newborn genetic screening. To avoid giving the state health department their child's blood or genetic test results, some parents opt out of the testing altogether, even if they would like their child tested.

This "rock and a hard place" decision forces parents to choose between the risk of not finding out early that their child has a rare newborn condition and the risk of government genetic profiling, which increasingly includes government ownership of their child's DNA.

For these reasons and perhaps for other reasons as well, some parents with the right to opt out of testing are opting out in greater numbers. As the specter of eugenics rises publicly over the program, the refusal rate is expected to increase.

Genetic Registries Emerge

Newborn genetic screening is done at state health department laboratories. Hospitals send newborn blood on a special card to the health department. The test results are then sent to the infant's physician. Some states—perhaps all states—register newborn test results in a state database. The Minnesota Department of Health database holds the newborn genetic test results of all children born since July 1, 1986—more than 1.5 million children. Although the database is referred to as the newborn screening database, this database is essentially a state genetic registry filled with hereditary data. There can be no doubt that newborn genetic screening is focused on hereditary-based disorders. The titles of state newborn genetic screening laws tell the story:

- *Screening for metabolic disorders, other hereditary and congenital disorders, and environmental risk factors* (FLORIDA)

- *Hereditary and Congenital Disorders Programs* (MARYLAND)

- *Tests of Infants for Heritable and Congenital Disorders* (MINNESOTA)

- *Phenylketonuria, Other Heritable Diseases, Hypothyroidism, and Certain Other Disorders* (TEXAS)

- *Phenylketonuria and other preventable heritable disorders* (WASHINGTON)

State government registration of genetic information on children—and their family bloodlines—is of particular concern given the history of how such registries have been used in the past for eugenic purposes. [Holocaust historian Susan Bachrach notes that Adolf] Hitler's [Nazi] regime had hundreds of "hereditary and racial care clinics" that examined family histories and "created vast hereditary data banks for the regimes' future use." Many state health departments already have cancer registries, birth defect registries, stroke registries and myriad other government patient databases. Most are electronic, linkable and searchable. As we are reminded by the American Society of Human Genetics: "The Nazi sterilization program owed part of its success to the efficiency with which the government maintained patient registries, which made it comparatively easy to locate persons with various disorders."

The Collection of Baby DNA

Public health agencies not only collect genetic testing data, they collect DNA—the baby's blood. Hospitals are required to send more blood to the agency than is needed for the testing. This *over-collection* provides health officials with a rich supply of citizen DNA that some states are already using for research without consent. The Hastings Center explains the connection:

> "Because only a fraction of each blood sample taken for newborn screening is used in the screening, the remainder is a valuable potential resource for research and program evaluation."

Twenty states store newborn blood samples from one to 23 years. With 4 million babies born each year and at least ten states retaining newborn blood indefinitely, the repository of infant DNA is large and growing. The baby's DNA is considered state government property. According to the book *The Stored Tissue Issue* [by Robert F. Weir, Robert S. Olick, and Jeffrey C. Murray], there are currently "more than 13.5 million newborn screening cards in storage and new cards being stored at a rate of 10,000–500,000 cards a year, depending on state populations." Most parents have no idea this is happening.

However, a recent University of Michigan study found that parents are opposed to government storage of newborn blood spots (NBS) and the use of baby DNA for research without parent consent: "A majority of parents are willing to have their children's NBS samples used for research—if their permission is obtained." The study concluded, "Using NBS samples for research without obtaining permission [is] not palatable to parents." . . .

All citizens, including newborns, have the right not to become involuntary subjects of genetic research.

Involuntary Genetic Research

Despite parent opposition, government health officials and others say infant DNA is critical to genetic research and essential to the development of new newborn genetic screening tests. State officials also claim a repository of baby DNA is necessary for the improvement of public health. Those who oppose the retention and use of newborn DNA without parent consent are said to be engaging in "social terrorism."

These kinds of statements disregard the DNA property rights and human civil rights of citizens. Genetic research and development of newborn genetic screening tests is genetic research on children and their family bloodlines. Although some state officials prefer to call test development "public health studies" or "newborn screening studies," *test development is genetic research*. One newborn test development project in Texas is said to cost more than $1,000,000 just to finish the project. Clearly, this is research. All citizens, including newborns, have the right not to become involuntary subjects of genetic research. . . .

The Issue of Privacy

The government's newborn genetic test results are not private. They become part of a government record in some if not all states. The results are also sent to the baby's physician for entry into the child's permanent medical record—likely to be electronic and available online.

In addition, the results are available under the so-called federal HIPAA [Health Insurance Portability and Accountability Act] "privacy" rule, to more than 600,000 entities including government agencies. Private insurers and Medicaid officials—who may be responsible for reimbursing hospitals for the cost of newborn genetic screening—may also have access to the test results. Furthermore, although most parents don't realize it, the child's newborn genetic screening results can disclose a portion of the *parent's* genetic profile, including some indication of whether the parent is a carrier of one or more genetic traits.

It is not hard to imagine the day when any discovered but non-symptomatic condition could become a "pre-existing condition" for which private insurers would not pay. The eugenic implications are obvious. Thus, the growing collection of genetic test results and newborn DNA could easily enable a eugenic agenda on the part of government agencies and private industry. . . .

The Need for Informed Consent

In light of the continued expansion of state newborn genetic screening programs, state retention of newborn DNA, government registration of newborn genetic test results, and concerns about the reemergence of eugenics, informed written parent consent requirements are needed for the protection of all citizens including newborn citizens. Prior to expanding state newborn genetic screening programs to include genetic testing of babies for common conditions and adult-onset diseases, state legislators must protect citizens from eugenic strategies in and outside of state government. Specific protective strategies include:

- Allow parents to choose the conditions for which their child is tested

- Destruction of current state newborn DNA repositories

101

- Before newborn blood is taken, require informed written consent for:

  - Newborn genetic screening

  - Government storage of test results and newborn DNA

  - Research using newborn DNA and newborn genetic test results.

Finally, state legislatures should privatize newborn genetic screening programs to protect citizens from state genetic registries, state ownership of citizen DNA, government research projects, and intrusive government interference in private family and medical decisions.

Genetic Screening Can Have Unintended Consequences

Steve Olson

Steve Olson is a writer and the author of Mapping Human History: Genes, Race, and Our Common Origins.

A few months ago, I sat down at my desk to open a letter that could tell me whether my father was really my father. In fact, that letter could tell me whether the men going back 10 generations on my paternal side were the biological fathers of their children.

Genetic Testing

I wasn't caught up in some bizarre multigenerational paternity suit. A scientific officer at a genetic testing company knew that I was interested in genealogy, and he had offered to run my DNA through a sequencer. A few weeks earlier, I'd swished mouthwash inside my cheeks, scaled the mouthwash in a tube, and mailed the tube to the company.

My doughty Scandinavian ancestors passed the test. My DNA revealed no obvious instances where the man named on a birth certificate differed from the man who was my biological ancestor. But I was lucky. Many efforts to trace male ancestry using DNA terminate at what geneticists delicately call a "non-paternity event." According to Bennett Greenspan, whose company, Family Tree DNA, sponsors projects that attempt to link different families to common ancestors, "Any project that has more than 20 or 30 people in it is likely to have an *oops* in it."

The law of unintended consequences is about to catch up with the genetic testing industry. Geneticists and physicians

Steve Olson, "Who's Your Daddy? Your Father May Not Be Who You Think He Is," *Atlantic*, vol. 300, July-August 2007, pp. 36–37. Reproduced by permission of the author.

would like us all to have our DNA sequenced. That way we'll know about our genetic flaws, and this knowledge could let us take steps to prevent future health problems. But genetic tests can also identify the individuals from whom we got our DNA. Widespread genetic testing could reveal many uncomfortable details about what went on in our parents' and grandparents' bedrooms.

Non-Paternity Rates

The problem would not loom so large if non-paternity were rare. But it isn't. When geneticists do large-scale studies of populations, they sometimes can't help but learn about the paternity of the research subjects. They rarely publish their findings, but the numbers are common knowledge within the genetics community. In graduate school, genetics students typically are taught that 5 to 15 percent of the men on birth certificates are not the biological fathers of their children. In other words, as many as one of every seven men who proudly carry their newborn children out of a hospital could be a cuckold.

Men pass most of their Y chromosomes down to their sons intact and unadulterated.

Non-paternity rates appear to be substantially lower in some populations. The Sorenson Molecular Genealogy Foundation, which is based in Salt Lake City, now has a genetic and genealogical database covering almost 100,000 volunteers, with an overrepresentation of people interested in genealogy. The non-paternity rate for a representative sample of its father-son pairs is less than 2 percent. But other reputed non-paternity rates are higher than the canonical numbers. One unpublished study of blood groups in a town in southeastern England indicated that 30 percent of the town's husbands could not have been the biological fathers of their children.

Even with a low non-paternity rate, the odds increase with each successive generation. Given an average non-paternity rate of 5 percent, the chance of such an event occurring over 10 generations exceeds 40 percent.

Most people can't look that far back on their family trees, but I can. Someone on the Olson side of my family once spent an inordinate amount of time tracing the family's male lineage. My relative's genealogical research indicated that my father's father's father's father's father's father's father's father's father migrated from Finland to Norway in the middle of the 17th century. If that is the case, I have a particular connection to that man.

The Y Chromosome

Men pass most of their Y chromosomes down to their sons intact and unadulterated. I therefore have the same Y chromosome as my father, and his father, and so on. (In fact, all men living today have inherited the Y chromosome of a single man who lived about 50,000 years ago, probably in eastern Africa. But mutations have slowly changed the Y chromosome over many generations, which is why the Y chromosomes of Finns generally differ from those of Greeks. Nevertheless, over the course or 10 or even 100 generations, the changes typically are small and the heritage is clear.) The continuity of the Y chromosome is how we know that Thomas Jefferson almost certainly had children with his slave Sally Hemings: Her direct male descendants have the same Y chromosome as Jefferson's paternal uncle, who presumably had the same Y chromosome as Jefferson. (Similar tests can reveal whether sons and daughters are really descended from their mothers and grandmothers, though non-maternity is much rarer than non-paternity.)

My Y chromosome turned out to be as Finnish as sautéed reindeer—I almost certainly inherited it from that 17th-century Finnish émigré. But even if my Y chromosome had turned out to be suspiciously un-Finnish, I probably could have come up with a story to protect my legitimacy. I could have said that my Finnish ancestor was the descendant of a Mongolian invader, or the son of a trader from Istanbul, or even a Spanish diplomat fallen on hard times (though in fact I know that he was a peasant farmer). I could have said that one of the men in my paternal lineage was adopted after his mother and father died. The imagination is a wonderful balm for bruised expectations.

But genetic tests don't lie, which means that our imaginations may be in for a workout. For example, groups of people in many parts of the world trace their lineage to particularly prominent male ancestors. In some cases, genetic tests reveal a kernel of truth behind these stories. Genghis Khan's Y chromosome really is widely distributed in Asia, for instance. Still, many of these stories have social rather than genealogical roots. "Many times we romanticize about the different groups that we have ancestry with," says Rick Kittles, a geneticist at the University of Chicago who founded the company African Ancestry. When Kittles has told clients that their genetic tests don't coincide with what they believe, a few, he says, have been shattered.

The pressure to undergo genetic testing is about to increase.

The Pressure to Undergo Genetic Testing

Frankly, I hadn't thought much about these issues before sitting down to open that letter from the genetic testing company. If I had, I doubt I would have agreed to the test. If my Y chromosome was not what I expected, would I tell other family members about it—including my teenaged son? Would I have been tempted to encourage my brother, then my male cousins through my father's brothers, then my male second cousins through my grandfather's brothers, and so on to be tested so that I could determine where the non-paternity occurred? I think we'd all have been better off assuming the best and shunning the test.

But the pressure to undergo genetic testing is about to increase. New technologies are reducing the cost of sequencing DNA. Researchers are now establishing extensive databases of DNA sequences combined with health information so they can link specific genes to diseases. And once the contributions of our genes to common diseases are discovered, everyone could benefit from DNA testing. Already, the Personal Genome Project at Harvard University is seeking volunteers who are willing to have their DNA sequences and medical information posted on the Web for biomedical purposes, even though the project warns that a person's DNA could be used to "infer paternity or other features of the volunteer's genealogy."

Two of the men most responsible for the sequencing of the human genome—James Watson and [John] Craig Venter—are making most of their genomes available on the Web. But if their sons ever decide to have their DNA tested, they could face the same situation I did in opening that letter. Watson has kept part of his genome private because he doesn't want his sons and the public to know whether he has a genetic variant predisposing him to Alzheimer's disease; he seems unconcerned about what the rest might reveal.

In the absence of stringent and possibly unattainable privacy protections, widespread testing will lead to many unpleasant surprises.

The Issue of Non-Paternity

Genetic counselors have been struggling with the issue of non-paternity for years. When a child is born with a genetic disorder, the parents may go to a counselor to learn whether they should try to have more children. If tests reveal that the presumed father of the child is not the biological father, most counselors will tell only the mother. But a vocal minority insists that paternity should be known to all.

So far, the expense of these tests has limited their use to cases like the one above, where a serious genetic disorder is already apparent. But what will happen when people begin sequencing large parts of their DNA routinely, to see whether they are vulnerable to specific diseases? If you discovered a predisposition to heart attacks or prostate cancer, and medications could reduce your vulnerability, wouldn't you want to tell your siblings and cousins? And shouldn't they be tested, too? Yet in the absence of stringent and possibly unattainable privacy protections, widespread testing will lead to many unpleasant surprises.

Geneticists have only begun to think about how to protect people from knowing themselves too well. But they probably should have seen this problem coming a long time ago. An oft-quoted definition of their field is: "Genetics explains why you look like your father—and if you don't, why you should."

CHAPTER 3

Should People Be Free to Pursue Genetic Enhancement?

Overview:
Genetic Enhancement

Kathi E. Hanna

Kathi E. Hanna is senior vice president and section head for science at Styllus, LLC, a medical and scientific writing company.

In general, genetic enhancement refers to the transfer of genetic material intended to modify non-pathological human traits. The term commonly is used to describe efforts to make someone not just well, but better than well, by optimizing attributes or capabilities—perhaps by raising an individual from standard to peak levels of performance. When the goal is enhancement, the gene may supplement the functioning of normal genes or may be superseded with genes that have been engineered to produce a desired enhancement. Furthermore, gene insertion may be intended to affect a single individual through somatic cell modification, or it may target the gametes, in which case the resulting effect could be passed on to succeeding generations.

In a sense, the concept of genetic enhancement is not particularly recent if one considers genetically engineered drug products used to alter physical traits as genetic enhancements. For example, human growth hormone (HGH), which before 1985 could be obtained only in limited quantities from cadaveric pituitary glands, now can be produced using recombinant DNA technology. When its supply was more limited, HGH was prescribed for children with short stature caused by classical growth hormone deficiency. However, with the advent of recombinant DNA manufacturing, some physicians have begun recommending use of HGH for nonhormone-deficient children who are below normal height.

Kathi E. Hanna, "Genetic Enhancement," National Human Genome Research Institute, National Institutes of Health, April 2006. www.genome.gov.

Animal Experiments

Animal experiments to date have attempted to improve such traits as growth rate or muscle mass. Although this research is focused on developing approaches to treating human diseases and conditions, it is conceivable that developments resulting from this research could be more broadly applied to enhance traits rather than correct deficiencies.

Recently, *Schwarzenegger mice* have been bred—laboratory animals whose bodies have expanded rapidly after the injection of a gene that causes muscles to grow. The mice are the first stage in the development of treatments intended to coax the bodies of seriously ill patients with degenerating diseases to recreate damaged tissue (e.g., muscular dystrophy). In the world of sports, this technology could potentially be used to improve athletic performance without being detected.

Similar interventions could help delay the aging process. For example, a gene called MGF (mechano growth factor) regulates a naturally occurring hormone produced after exercise that stimulates muscle production. Levels of MGF fall as we age, which is one reason why muscle mass is lost as we grow older. A treatment to build up muscles would allow us to remain able-bodied and independent much longer. IGF-1, another muscle-building hormone, has produced increased muscle mass in laboratory mice. Theoretically, gene insertion of IGF-1 could produce an equally impressive effect in humans.

Efforts to genetically improve the growth of swine have involved the insertion of transgenes encoding growth hormone. Nevertheless, despite the fact that growth hormone transgenes are expressed well in swine, increased growth does not occur. Another effort aimed to enhance muscle mass in cattle. When gene transfer was accomplished, the transgenic calf initially exhibited muscle hypertrophy, but muscle degeneration and wasting soon followed and the animal had to be destroyed.

Gene transfer at the embryonic stage through a technique called pronuclear microinjection is another approach being tested in animals. However, current knowledge from animal experiments suggests that embryo gene transfer is unsafe, as its use results in random integration of donor DNA, a lack of control of the number of gene copies inserted, significant rearrangements of host genetic material, and a 5 to 10 percent frequency of insertional mutagenesis. In addition, this technique would necessarily be followed by nuclear transfer into enucleated oocytes [immature eggs], a process that in at least two animal models is associated with a low birth rate and a very high rate of late pregnancy loss or newborn death. Thus, many believe that the use of gene transfer at the embryonic stage for enhancement would reach far beyond the limits of acceptable medical intervention.

The state of knowledge in humans and other complex organisms does not allow for the controlled genetic modification of even simple phenotypes.

The Complexity of Humans

Greater success has been achieved in genetic enhancement of plants, which are more easily manipulated genetically and reproductively. However, the state of knowledge in humans and other complex organisms does not allow for the controlled genetic modification of even simple phenotypes.

For example, in humans, for whom more complex traits such as intelligence or behavior are concerned, the limitations are more pronounced. The genome provides only a blueprint for formation of the brain. The complex and subtle details of assembly and intellectual development involve more than direct genetic control and are subject to inestimable stochastic [random] and environmental influences. Despite the technical limitations, it is possible that eventually enhancements using techniques initially intended to restore deficiencies could be redirected to improve memory and problem solving, reduce the need for sleep, increase musical capacity, attain desirable personality traits, protect against cardiovascular disease or cancer, or increase longevity.

One of the areas in which genetic enhancement might find initial application is in sports. At the 1964 Winter Olympics in Innsbruck, [Austria], a cross-country skier from Finland who won two gold medals was later found to have a genetic mutation that increased the number of red blood cells in his body because he could not switch off erythropoietin (EPO) production. This mutation increased the athlete's capacity for aerobic exercise. A synthetic version of EPO is currently used to treat anemia, but it has also been abused by athletes to heighten their stamina. For example, in the 1998 Tour de France, a team was thrown out of the race, and two top cyclists admitted taking the drug. Recent efforts to deliver the EPO gene into patients' cells would eliminate the need for regular injections, but this process could also be abused by athletes.

Ethical Concerns

Genetic enhancement raises a host of ethical, legal and social questions. What is meant by normal? When is a genetic intervention "enhancing" or "therapeutic"? How should the benefit from a genetic enhancement be calculated in comparing its risks and benefits? Would people who have been genetically enhanced enjoy an unfair advantage in competing for scarce resources? That is, will genetic enhancement be available to all or only to the few who can afford to purchase it using their personal finances? These questions relate to the two major concerns presented by genetic enhancement: the undermining of the principle of social equality and the problem of creating an unfair advantage that would be enjoyed by enhanced individuals.

Some have speculated that genetic enhancement might affect human evolution. Philosophical and religious objections also have been raised, based on the belief that to intervene in such fundamental biological processes is "playing God" or attempting to place us above God. People from various perspectives believe that any interference with the random offerings of nature is inherently wrong and question our right to toy with the product of years of natural selection. Geneticists have countered that the power to control human evolution is unlikely, as the evolution of the human species is a nonrandom change in allelic frequencies resulting from selective pressure. The change progresses over generations because individuals with specific patterns of alleles [alternative forms of a gene, existing in pairs on a specific site on a chromosome] are favored reproductively. If new alleles were introduced by gene transfer, the impact on the species would be negligible. Moreover, there is no certainty that genetically enhanced individuals would have greater biological fitness, as measured by reproductive success.

Although the distinctions between cure and enhancement might be obvious to some, they can lose meaning in medical practice or in formulating health policy.

In general, however, ethical and social concerns center not so much on the improvement of traits for alleviation of deficiencies or on the reduction of disease risk, but on the augmentation of functions that without intervention would be considered entirely normal. For some individuals, technologies that can enhance traits are even more attractive than those that would merely duplicate them (e.g., cloning). And, although the distinctions between cure and enhancement might be obvious to some, they can lose meaning in medical practice or in formulating health policy. For example, interventions that begin in an effort to cure could slide quickly toward interventions that enhance.

Enhancement techniques are likely to emerge as unapproved or off-label uses of approved products, uses over which FDA lacks effective regulatory control.

Regulatory Issues

The questions raised above also create significant new challenges to our regulatory capabilities.

On September 11, 1997, the National Institutes of Health (NIH) convened a conference on genetic enhancement. The meeting was prompted by a request to NIH to approve a protocol for conducting a gene therapy experiment on healthy volunteers, rather than on patients. Although the experiment was part of an effort to develop treatments for cystic fibrosis, the proposed use of healthy subjects raised, for the first time, the questions of whether and in what circumstances it was appropriate to use gene insertion technology in healthy volunteers. Exactly how to regulate this potential use of genetic technology remains unclear.

In order for the Food and Drug Administration (FDA) to control the introduction and use of genetic enhancement technologies, these techniques would have to be considered to be drugs, biologics, or medical devices, categories for which FDA has the authority to regulate genetic enhancements. Regarding drugs used for enhancement purposes, the definition of a drug in the Federal Food, Drug, and Cosmetic Act includes not only "articles intended for use in the diagnosis, cure, mitigation, treatment, or prevention of disease in man" but also "articles (other than food) intended to affect the structure or function of the body of man." The agency has relied on this definition to assert drug regulatory authority over products such as wrinkle creams and tanning agents that are intended to enhance the appearance of the body but that achieve results by affecting the body's structural or functional components. The agency will be challenged by the need to determine when enhancement is "genetic" (versus nongenetic, for example, liposuction or cosmetic surgery) and when genetic manipulation is "enhancement." In addition, FDA's ability to regulate genetic enhancements in the traditional areas of safety and efficacy will be put to the test by data deficiencies and the subjectivity of judgments about risk and benefit. In addition, enhancement techniques are likely to emerge as unapproved or off-label uses of approved products, uses over which FDA lacks effective regulatory control.

Genetic Enhancement Should Only Be Limited by Regulations for Safety and Efficacy

Ronald Bailey

Ronald Bailey is a science correspondent for Reason *magazine and Reason.com, where he writes a weekly science and technology column. He is the author of* Liberation Biology: The Scientific and Moral Case for the Biotech Revolution.

What is transhumanism? A pretty good definition is offered by bioethicist and transhumanist James Hughes who states that transhumanism is "the idea that humans can use reason to transcend the limitation of the human condition." Specifically, transhumanists welcome the development of intimate technologies that will enable people to boost their life spans, enhance their intellectual capacities, augment their athletic abilities, and choose their preferred emotional states. What's particularly noteworthy is that Hughes argues that democratic decision making is central to the task of guiding humanity into the transhuman future. . . .

Restrictions on Reproductive Technologies

The urge for democratically imposed restrictions on the use of reproductive technologies has not abated. Recall that the federal government imposed a moratorium in the 1970s on funding any research on in vitro fertilization [IVF] techniques. In January 1980, Sen. Orrin Hatch (R-Utah), alarmed by the opening of the first IVF clinic in the United States, sent a letter to Sen. Ted Kennedy (D-Mass.), who was then chairman of

Ronald Bailey, "Transhumanism and the Limits of Democracy: A Paper Presented at the Workshop on Transhumanism and Democracy," *Reason*, April 28, 2009. Reproduced by permission.

a health and scientific research subcommittee, urging him to convene hearings on the grounds that "prudence and our commitment to public participation in decision making suggest that the test tube baby laboratory not become fully operational until we have had the opportunity to consider the matter in open congressional hearings." Nine states including New York currently prohibit gestational surrogacy.

In 1993, President Bill Clinton rejected the recommendations from the NIH's [National Institutes of Health's] Human Embryo Research Panel and prohibited federal funding of the creation of human embryos solely for research purposes. This ban did not apply to research on spare embryos or privately funded research. In addition, in the wake of the announcement that Scottish researchers had cloned a sheep in 1997, President Clinton announced an immediate moratorium on any human cloning research. In 1998, Clinton urged Congress to ban human cloning experiments for at least five years. Today [2009] 13 states ban reproductive human cloning, and six outlaw therapeutic cloning. The House of Representatives twice passed a bill that would have criminalized somatic cell nuclear transfer research and which would have criminalized any American who went abroad to take advantage of therapies developed using that technique—the penalty would have been 10 years in prison and $1 million in fines. . . .

Democratically imposed restrictions on using advanced biotechnological techniques are not confined to the United States. For example, Britain established the Human Fertilisation and Embryology Authority (HFEA) in 1991 to regulate the use of embryos and gametes in infertility treatment and research. The HFEA has told couples that they could not select the sex of embryos to be implanted.

Even now, parents wanting to use PGD [preimplantation genetic diagnosis] to ensure that their children will not be burdened with an inherited genetic disease must apply for permission from the HFEA. And the HFEA has banned paying women for providing eggs to be used in research. Crucially, the HFEA can regulate not just on the grounds of ensuring quality, safety, and efficacy, but also on ethical grounds.

An Example of Government Interference

Consider the case of the Whitaker family from Sheffield, England, to see just how perilous it is to allow a government agency to interfere in a family's reproductive decisions. In 2002, Michelle and Jayson Whitaker asked the HFEA for permission to use in vitro fertilization and PGD to produce a tissue-matched sibling for their son Charlie, who suffers from a rare anemia. That disease caused him to need a blood transfusion every three weeks. The HFEA refused, calling the procedure "unlawful and unethical," ruling that tissue matching is not a sufficient reason to attempt embryo selection. Desperate, the Whitakers came to the United States, where PGD is still legal. In June 2003, Michelle Whitaker gave birth to James, whose umbilical cord stem cells are immunologically compatible with Charlie's. The stem cells were transplanted and, six years later, both boys are reported to be healthy. Please keep in mind that taking stem cells from James's umbilicus in no way endangered or harmed him.

Again, in this case, the HFEA's refusal was not based on safety or efficacy, but on the moral opinions of the authority's governing panel. Such a regulatory authority necessarily turns differences over morality into win/lose propositions, with minority views—and rights—overridden by the majority.

It is hard to see what is ethically wrong with parents taking advantage of such testing, since it is aimed at conferring general benefits that any child would want to have.

Fortunately, Americans are allowed to use PGD to select "savior siblings" like James Whitaker and also to enable their progeny to avoid the risks of genetic diseases. For example, consider the 2002 case of a married 30-year-old geneticist who will almost certainly lose her mind to early-onset Alzheimer's disease by age 40 and who chose to have her embryos tested in vitro for the disease gene. She then implanted only embryos without the gene into her womb. The result was the birth of a healthy baby girl—one who will not suffer Alzheimer's in her 40s. The mother in this case certainly knows what would face any child of hers born with the disease gene. Her father, a sister, and a brother have all already succumbed to early Alzheimer's.

Not one of you *gave your consent to be born, much less to be born with the specific complement of genes that you bear.*

Social Consequences

Bioethicist Jeffrey Kahn objected to using PGD in this case arguing, "It's a social decision. This really speaks to the need for a larger policy discussion, and regulation or some kind of oversight of assisted reproduction." Kahn is right that parents will someday use PGD to screen embryos for desirable traits such as tougher immune systems, stronger bodies, and smarter brains. It is hard to see what is ethically wrong with parents taking advantage of such testing, since it is aimed at conferring general benefits that any child would want to have. . . .

Kahn is wrong when he claims that the decision to use PGD by prospective parents is a "social decision" requiring more regulation. First of all, in the capacious sense implied by Kahn, any parent's decision to have a child, even by conventional means, has "social consequences" for us all. So would Kahn have neighbors, regulators, and bioethicists weigh in on everybody's reproductive decisions? Kahn would doubtless

counter that, unlike conventional reproduction, assisted reproduction involves the use of scarce medical resources that could
be used for other purposes (which they prefer).

Again, Kahn's notion of "social" could apply to anything—
what if Kahn disapproved of someone buying nonunion cloth-
ing or vacationing in the Caribbean rather than devoting his
resources to building public parks or highways? In this case,
the parents using assisted reproduction and PGD are spending
their own money for the benefit of their own children to
work with doctors who are freely devoting their skills.

The Consent of Children-To-Be

Another often-heard objection is that genetic engineering will
be imposed on "children-to-be" without their consent. First, I
need to remind everyone reading this article *that not one of
you* gave your consent to be born, much less to be born with
the specific complement of genes that you bear. Thus, the
children born by means of assisted reproductive therapies and
those produced more conventionally stand in exactly the same
ethical relationship to their parents. [German philosopher Jür-
gen] Habermas disagrees, claiming, "Eugenic interventions
aiming at enhancement reduce ethical freedom insofar as they
tie down the person concerned to rejected, but irreversible in-
tentions of third parties, barring him from the spontaneous
self-perception of being the undivided author of his own life."
However, [philosophy professor] Allen Buchanan correctly
points out that Habermas does not actually make clear why a
person who develops from a genetically enhanced embryo
should feel that they are not the "author" of her life or be re-
garded as being somehow less free by others. Habermas "is assuming that how one's genome was selected is relevant to
one's moral status as a person. This error is no less fundamental than thinking that a person's pedigree—for example,

whether she is of noble blood or 'base-born'—determines her moral status," explains Buchanan.

Another frequently heard assertion from opponents of enhancement technologies is that a genetically engineered child somehow feels less loved and appreciated than one who was born in the conventional way. Similar fears were expressed by many bioethicists when in vitro fertilization began to be used in the 1970s and 1980s. The good news is that recent research finds that IVF children and their parents are as well-adjusted as those born in the conventional way. And this should be the case for enhanced children as well. As Frances Kamm [professor of philosophy and public policy] argues, "Not accepting whatever characteristics nature will bring but altering them ex-ante does not show lack of love. . . . This is because no conscious being yet exists who has to work hard to achieve new traits or suffer fears of rejection at the idea they should be changed. Importantly, it is rational and acceptable to seek good characteristics in a new person, even though we know when the child comes to be and we love him or her, many of these characteristics may come and go and we will continue to love the particular person."

The absurdity of a requirement for prenatal consent becomes transparent when you ask proponents of such a requirement if they would forbid fetal surgery to correct spina bifida or fetal heart defects. After all, those fetuses can't give their consent to those procedures, yet it is certainly the moral thing to do. For that matter, taking this strong position on consent to its logically extreme conclusion would mean that children couldn't be treated with drugs, or receive vaccinations. So using future biotechnical means to correct genetic diseases like cystic fibrosis or sickle-cell anemia at the embryonic stage will similarly be morally laudatory activity. Surely one can assume that the beneficiary—the not-yet-born, possibly even the not-yet-conceived child—would happily have chosen to have those diseases corrected.

Consent for Enhancement

But what about enhancements, not just therapeutic biotechnical interventions? Let's say a parent could choose genes that would guarantee her child a 20 point IQ boost. It is reasonable to presume that the child would be happy to consent to this enhancement of her capacities. How about plugging in genes that would boost her immune system and guarantee that she would never get colon cancer, Alzheimer's, AIDS, or the common cold? Again, it seems reasonable to assume consent. These enhancements are general capacities that any human being would reasonably want to have. In fact, lots of children already do have these capacities naturally, so it's hard to see that there is any moral justification for outlawing access to them for others.

Fritz Allhoff [assistant professor of philosophy] has grappled nicely with the issue of consent. Allhoff offers a principle derived from the second formulation of [German philosopher Immanuel] Kant's categorical imperative that we treat individuals as ends and never merely as means or, more simply, to treat them in ways to which they would rationally consent. Allhoff turns next to philosopher John Rawls's notion of primary goods. In *A Theory of Justice*, Rawls defines primary goods as those goods that every rational person should value, regardless of his conception of the good. These goods include rights, liberties, opportunities, health, intelligence, and imagination. As Allhoff argues, "These are the things that, *ex hypothesi*, everyone should want; it would be *irrational* to turn them down when offered. Nobody could be better off with less health or with fewer talents, for example, regardless of her life goals. . . . Since primary goods are those that, by definition, any rational agent would want regardless of his conception of the good, *all rational agents would consent to augmentation of their primary goods."*

Allhoff then contends that such enhancements would be permissible if every future generation would consent to them. But the requirement that all future generations must consent adds nothing to the moral force of Allhoff's arguments since already all rational agents would consent to such enhancements. So again, safe genetic interventions that improve a prospective child's health, cognition, and so forth would be morally permissible because we can presume consent from the individuals who benefit from the enhancements.

With accumulation of genetic understanding, human freedom will then properly be seen as acting to overcome these predispositions.

Genes and Freedom

Many opponents of human genetic engineering are either conscious or unconscious genetic determinists. They fear that biotechnological knowledge and practice will somehow undermine human freedom. In a sense, these genetic determinists believe that somehow human freedom resides in the gaps of our knowledge of our genetic makeup. If parents are allowed to choose their children's genes, then they will have damaged their children's autonomy and freedom. According to environmentalist Bill McKibben, "The person left without any choice *at all* [emphasis his] is the one you've engineered. You've decided, for once and for all, certain things about him: He'll have genes expressing proteins that send extra dopamine to alter his mood; he'll have genes expressing proteins to boost his memory; to shape his stature." People like McKibben apparently believe that our freedom and autonomy somehow depend on the unknown and random combinations of genes that a person inherits. But even if they were right—and they are not—genetic ignorance of this type will not last.

Advances in human whole genome testing will likely become available by 2014 so that every person's entire complement of genes can be scanned and known at his or her physician's office for as little as $1,000. Once whole genome testing is perfected we will all learn what even our randomly conferred genes may predispose us to do and from what future ills we are likely to suffer. Already, my relatively inexpensive genotype scan from 23andMe tells me that I have alleles that give me a somewhat greater risk of developing celiac disease, a lower risk of rheumatoid arthritis, as well as having a higher sensitivity to warfarin, among other traits. With accumulation of genetic understanding, human freedom will then properly be seen as acting to overcome these predispositions, much like a former alcoholic can overcome his thirst for booze. Fortunately, biotech will help here as well as with the development of neuropharmaceuticals to enhance our cognitive abilities and change our moods. . . .

Respecting Our Pluralistic Society

People should not be forced to use medicines and technologies that they find morally objectionable. Take the case of the Amish. Amish individuals live in an open society—ours—and can opt out of our society or theirs whenever they want. As followers of a reasonable comprehensive doctrine, they have a system for voluntarily deciding among themselves what new technologies they will embrace. The situation of the Amish demonstrates that technological choices don't have to involve everyone in a given society. (Although Amish practicality has caused them to embrace modern medicine when it comes to treating genetic maladies that plague their community.)

Eventually, one can imagine that in the future different treatment and enhancement regimens will be available to accommodate the different values and beliefs held by citizens.

Christian scientists would perhaps reject most of modern biotechnology outright; Jehovah's Witnesses might remain leery
of treatments that they interpret to being akin to using blood
products or blood transfusions; Roman Catholics might refuse
to use regenerative treatments derived from human embryonic stem cells; and still others will wish to take the fullest advantage of all biomedical enhancements and treatments. In
this way, a pluralistic society respects the reasonable comprehensive doctrines of their fellow citizens and enables social
peace among moral strangers.

---

*To the extent that new biotechnologies need regulation,
agencies should be limited to deciding, as they have traditionally done, only questions about safety and efficacy.*

[Bioethicist] Julian Savulescu is right when he reminds us,
"The Nazis sought to interfere directly in people's reproductive decisions (by forcing them to be sterilized) to promote
social ideals, particularly around racial superiority. Not offering selection for non-disease genes would indirectly interfere
(by denying choice) to promote social ideals such as equality
or 'population welfare.' There is no relevant difference between direct and indirect eugenics. The lesson we learned
from eugenics is that society should be loath to interfere
(directly and indirectly) in reproductive decision making."

The Role of Regulation

To the extent that new biotechnologies need regulation, agencies should be limited to deciding, as they have traditionally
done, only questions about safety and efficacy. Regulatory
agencies also have an important role in protecting research
subjects and patients from force and fraud by imposing informed consent requirements on researchers. But when people
of good will deeply disagree on moral issues that don't involve
the prevention of force or fraud, it is a fraught exercise to

submit their disagreement to a panel of political appointees or a democratic vote. That way leads to intolerance, repression, and social conflict.

The genius of a liberal society is that its citizens have wide scope to pursue their own visions of the good, including transhumanism, without excessive hindrance by their fellow citizens.

Genetic Enhancement Should Be Left to Personal Choice

Melvin Konner

Melvin Konner is the Samuel Candler Dobbs Professor of Anthropology and associate professor of psychiatry and neurology at Emory University.

Most religious traditions today not only accept advances in medical science but regard them in some sense as a moral imperative. Christians say, "God helps those who help themselves," Jews are urged to "repair the world" (and even to complete the work of creation), and the Dalai Lama famously reveres science and expresses doubts about elements in his own great religious tradition [Buddhism] when they seem to conflict with science's findings.

Religion and Medical Science

This was not always the case. Medieval Catholic clerics warned that medical treatment betrayed a lack of faith and deemed it incompatible with holy orders. Edward Jenner's invention of inoculation, in the 1790s, met with wide religious condemnation on both sides of the Atlantic on the grounds that inoculation usurped God's power over life and death, and that only hypocrites could accept it and still pray. The 19th-century Scottish Calvinist church reviled the use of chloroform to assuage the pain of childbirth as a "Satanic invention" that subverted God's design.

Like Prometheus [Greek mythological champion of humankind], Jenner gave humanity a new kind of power—and, for most of history, the Christian God could apparently be of-

Melvin Konner, "Our Bodies, Our Choices," *American Prospect*, vol. 18, May 2007, pp. 37–41. Copyright © 2007 The American Prospect, Inc. All rights reserved. Reproduced with permission from *The American Prospect*, 11 Beacon Street, Suite 1120, Boston, MA 02108.

fended just as Zeus could. But today only a few medical Luddites [persons opposed to technological change] think Jenner burns in hell; most believers think of him and other medical scientists as God's assistant healers, something like the residents in a surgical suite handing the senior surgeon instruments and closing up after the serious work is done.

Still, this history, in which right-thinking clergy deemed the greatest advances in medicine the greatest affronts to God, is instructive. Then, as now, some scientists were "playing God," egregiously trying to control life and death, to tinker with birth, pain, and suffering—God's business, if anything is—and thereby undermining not just faith but the order of the world.

Control of biological processes is greater than ever, and will be greater still.

Many argue that today is different, and in some ways it is. Control of biological processes is greater than ever, and will be greater still. In many species, genes can be knocked out and socked in, and a growing Noah's ark of animals can be cloned. Cells can be sucked from early embryos and, perhaps, turned into engines of organ repair. Few mothers need to ask, "Is it a boy or a girl?" in the delivery room, as prenatal knowledge becomes universal and deliberate opting for one or the other sex becomes more common. Sperm banks give women or couples control over countless characteristics of their not-yet-conceived unborn offspring, and, through in vitro fertilization, choice is possible even when the egg and sperm are your own. Growth hormone makes short children taller whether or not they have a deficiency, and eventually an inserted gene will boost their own supply.

Surely a God with the power to make even kings tremble must be glaring down on all of this, thinking *enough is enough*. Or at least there must be a troubled inner voice raising some fundamental moral questions. Michael Sandel certainly hears that voice. A Harvard political philosopher and former member of President [George W.] Bush's Council on Bioethics, he has written a book of reflections—a meditative essay, really—on the moral questions raised by these new technologies, among others. In general, he is uncomfortable with the technologies and, like the members of the president's council, he holds firm opinions against them. I find neither his arguments nor theirs persuasive.

Nongenetic Enhancement

Despite the subtitle—*Ethics in the Age of Genetic Engineering*—much of *The Case Against Perfection* goes beyond genetics. A sports enthusiast, Sandel asks if extraneous enhancements—whether steroids or genes—are in the spirit of the game. Aren't we looking for truly human competition, human excellence? Don't the medical adulterations take that away?

Perhaps, and certainly the arbiters of the games are trying to keep bio-finagling at bay. But Sandel himself observes that shoes were once thought adulterants of the skills of track and field. Do we think that the millions who pay good money to watch Barry Bonds slug away at 98-mile-an-hour pitches are fools to do so because of the steroid scandal? Or do they just not care as much as bioethicists think they should?

There is no intrinsic difference between inserting genes and inserting steroids.

When I watch basketball giants jumping to score points from an 11-foot height, knowing that the tallest men of the past reached perhaps 6 feet, am I watching human or superhuman players? When I consider that the best football players of 1920 could not survive on a modern gridiron, do I think that scientific methods of coaching, selection, nutrition, and exercise have violated the essence of the sport? Drugs are different, but, having no crystal ball nor being able to read the minds of hundreds of millions of sports fans, I don't know whether steroids will be successfully forbidden. Time and sports fans will tell. Perhaps one day there will be parallel halls of fame for "enhanced" and "naked" versions of the games.

We see the phrase "gene manipulation" and think we are in a Frankensteinian realm that has never existed before. In a technical sense that is so. But more fundamentally, there is no intrinsic difference between inserting genes and inserting steroids—steroids work by turning genes on anyway—as long as the inserted genes are targeting muscle and bone, not eggs and sperm. The manipulation of genes in muscle and bone is a form of medication, legitimate or otherwise. Yes, there is a new technical principle involved, but it's still basically medication.

Growth hormone works well, and it could conceivably raise the ante of height in basketball if an eager sports-minded parent of a 6-foot-tall middle school player gets his or her hands on it. But should the coach turn away a talented kid because his father got him growth hormone injections? Or will the alumni still pay to see the slam dunk?

Personal Choice

What else should moral philosophers condemn? How about the nose job a beautiful friend of mine had as a teenager, which has made her feel a little phony ever since? How about the breast reduction one of my daughter's friends had recently because she was both embarrassed by the size of her chest and limited in athletics and dance? How about the people I know on Wellbutrin? Viagra?

Philosophy is a noble and heartfelt exercise, but life is life, and people enhance it—always have, always will. What it really comes down to in the end is personal choice. Do I think that should be limitless? No. But I am glad that when my daughter's friend talked with her parents and her doctor about her breasts, no philosophers showed up. If they were freely consulted, fine—but otherwise it's none of their business.

Genetic Enhancement

Now we come to something harder. Germ line therapy—tweaking genes in eggs and sperm—is different because those genes are forever. If you give me a gene as a teenager to bulk up my biceps, my kids may still be born weaklings. Tweak my sperm, and my babies will likely have big biceps, as will their babies, and theirs. This is a eugenics that eugenicists never dreamed of.

We have a version of it already. We can identify many genes we consider bad—for Tay-Sachs disease, say, or cystic fibrosis—and abort the fetuses, or select away the embryos during in vitro fertilization. Even antiabortion ethicists seem to have little trouble with the latter tactic. Few would shed any tears if Tay-Sachs, which horribly destroys the brain and kills before age 2, were never seen again. But consider bipolar and other mood disorders: Sufferers and their relatives tend to be more creative than average. If we eliminated bipolar genes, what else would we eliminate? The line between illness and variety is not always neatly drawn.

Sandel, like the bioethics council on which he served, takes a dim view of any form of enhancement. He casts a jaundiced eye on parents who put their kids in certain kindergartens to prime them for Princeton and Harvard, and on the notion of "a Viagra for the brain." I might think those parents foolish, but it's their kid and their money. And if a brain enhancer existed, at 60 I would go to the ends of the earth to get it.

One form of "genetic" enhancement especially irksome to Sandel is choosing eggs or sperm on the basis of the health, brains, and beauty of the donors. But this practice is little more than a technological extension of mate choice. Those who can have always chosen their mates—and therefore eggs or sperm—using the same criteria. Technology makes it different, but why not extend access to desirable qualities to those who, in the context of natural mate choice (discrimination in both senses of the word), cannot get them?

The new technologies dwell in a completely different moral universe.

We can't assume we know in advance the consequences of our newfound reproductive freedom. A sperm-sorting company helps prospective parents bias their chances for a boy or a girl; most customers want girls. And Sandel opens his book with the case of a deaf couple who wanted a deaf child and found a sperm donor with hereditary deafness. As the hearing child of deaf parents, I was saddened by the story, but I don't see it as very different morally from a deaf woman choosing that same man as her husband. Sandel opens the book with this case, apparently to shock us; in my view, however, all it does is highlight the fact that individual human beings make individual choices.

Eugenics and Coercion

Sandel, like most who oppose enhancement, improperly invokes the eugenics of the early 20th century (and even that of [Adolf] Hitler) to bolster his argument. But as he himself points out, the new technologies dwell in a completely different moral universe. A state-run, mandatory program of sterilization to cull the "unfit" against their will has nothing whatever to do with offering individuals options. After our last benighted century, few of us could countenance eugenics-by-mandate.

Reproductive technologies, however, are not about state coercion but about the opposite; the question is not whether the government will force them on me but whether the government, advised by Sandel and the Council on Bioethics, will step between me and my doctor and stop me from using them. Sandel's counterarguments—that compulsory use of genetic engineering could emerge someday, or that currents in the culture will exert a kind of coercion—are completely unconvincing. If he doesn't like the culture's idea of beauty or intelligence, let him change the culture. To his credit, he points out that moral philosophers as different as John Rawls, Robert Nozick, and Ronald Dworkin accept forms of genetic enhancement.

Gender selection in India is indeed worrisome: The proportion of females there is dropping precipitously, and the consequences a generation from now could be dire. But sex selection per se (as opposed to one of its methods, abortion) is a political-economic matter, not an ethical one. And as the great evolutionary theorist Ronald A. Fisher showed, skewed sex ratios right themselves as competition for the scarcer sex intensifies. In humans this will likely happen faster, as many parents who choose sons realize that they will have no grandchildren.

The Status of the Fetus

In an epilogue, Sandel briefly treats a truly ethical issue: the status of the fetus. If killing a fetus—whether for personal or research purposes—is killing a person, it is obviously wrong, and both state and church can intervene. The trouble is that we differ about whether a fetus is a person. President Bush and the council that serves at his pleasure are heavily biased on this issue against both abortion and stem cell research, but the majority of the country, as represented in polls and in Congress, has the opposite view. As Sandel points out, people who accord the fetus personhood are inconsistent: If destroying embryos is murder, embryonic wastage must be death. Where are the sacraments and the grieving for late menstrual periods, a large proportion of which contain early embryos?

Sandel favors embryonic stem cell research. But in any case, now as in the past, religious opposition will not retard legitimate science very much. California and other states, private corporations, and many nations are pressing ahead with this research—a consensus that perhaps should inform our ethics—and the main long-term effect of Bush's ban will be to export a few future Nobel Prizes.

Drawing the Line

Sandel wants us to be open to "the unbidden." But the unbidden used to include smallpox and crushing childbirth pain, and it still includes horrific genetic diseases. A line needs to be drawn somewhere between discarding a Tay-Sachs embryo and doing the same with one that will probably develop dementia at the end of a long, rewarding life. Philosophers make their most useful contribution when they clarify thought and language, and though Sandel does help clarify some of the issues, his book is replete with unconvincing moral judgments, much like the bioethics that is grounded in theology.

People use SAT prep courses and orthodontics to level the playing field for their children by eliminating irrelevant obstacles. We increasingly see Ritalin and Wellbutrin in a similar light, and we may go on to think the same of growth hormone. I see no intrinsic reason why gene therapy outside the germ line should be different. There will be errors like the big one we made with estrogen replacement, but they will be scientific errors, not ethical ones, and they will have scientific remedies.

As for our new and expanding suite of reproductive choices, many deem them a declaration of independence from evolution's caprices. If openness to "the unbidden" means the reproductive roulette that gave us Tay-Sachs, good riddance to it; I won't miss it one little bit. As for trying to eliminate stupidity and ugliness, it's fine for nice-looking intellectuals to tsk-tsk others, but if some want to give their children and grandchildren a different future, I won't be standing in their way.

The weightiest moral problem in the quest for perfection is that, at least under present circumstances, it increases inequality.

Are there hard choices ahead? Certainly. People must be taught the science, as in any genetic counseling. Eliminate the genes for sickle-cell anemia and you will decrease future generations' resistance to malaria. Eliminate those for bipolar disorder and you will find future generations less creative. Choose boys too often and you will increase crime and forgo grandchildren. These are in one sense ethical issues. We used antibiotics thoughtlessly with unfortunate results. The ethical path is not to stop using them but to use them more judiciously.

Addressing Inequality While Pursuing Perfection

There is one overarching ethical issue to which Sandel gives short shrift: inequality of access. He puts it aside because he wants to develop general moral rules for the procedures themselves. But the weightiest moral problem in the quest for perfection is that, at least under present circumstances, it increases inequality. Evolution itself is unfair enough without giving the fittest a technological boost. So there is a world of difference between a restricted quest for perfection and one open to everyone.

"[C]hanging our nature to fit the world," Sandel concludes, "deadens the impulse to social and political improvement. Rather than employ our new genetic powers to straighten 'the crooked timber of humanity,' we should do what we can to create social and political arrangements more hospitable to the gifts and limitations of imperfect human beings." Can't we walk and chew gum at the same time? I testified at a Senate hearing in favor of universal health care at the same time that I was paying to straighten my daughter's teeth.

"The crooked timber of humanity" means different things to different people, and we will be talking for generations, if not centuries, about how and how much to try to straighten it. But bioethicists should get off their high horses. Sandel is entitled to his opinions, but he is not entitled to mine. I have to ask myself not just how much perfection to seek but whether I want to live in a world where theologians and philosophers tell me how much I can have.

Humans Have a Right to Be Born Without Genetic Manipulation

Marcy Darnovsky

Marcy Darnovsky is associate executive director at the Center for Genetics and Society, an organization that encourages responsible uses and effective societal governance of genetic technologies.

Most people are well aware that efforts to "improve the human gene pool" and "breed better people," notoriously widespread from the end of the nineteenth century through the middle of the twentieth century, led to some of the most extreme violations of civil, political, and human rights in recent history. Nonetheless, five or six decades ago—before the structure of DNA had been deduced, before the modern environmental movement—most of the provisions of the Genetic Bill of Rights would have seemed nonsensical.

Even twenty-five years ago—before the development of genetic manipulation at the molecular level, legal doctrines that allow governments to grant patents on life, and DNA databases; before the advent and commercialization of in vitro fertilization and the screening of in vitro embryos; before the appearance of advertisements for social sex selection in mainstream U.S. publications—the document would have been widely considered an unwarranted overreaction based on dystopian fantasy.

New Genetic Technologies

But here we are, at the beginning of the twenty-first century. Plants and animals are routinely genetically modified, patented, and brought to market by corporate enterprises. Genetic technologies are increasingly applied to human beings for forensic and medical purposes. The biotechnology industry, though it has lost over $40 billion since its inception twenty-five years ago, continues to attract large amounts of venture capital and generate glowing headlines.

As many have observed, public understanding of these trends is lagging far behind technical developments and commercial deployment. Many people feel daunted by their technical complexity, and therefore reluctant to make political or ethical judgments about them. Grappling with the social meaning of the various human genetic technologies has proven thorny even for those whose political commitments usually make them wary of corporate-dominated technological projects.

More than a few observers predict that in vitro embryos will one day be manipulated and modified rather than merely screened and selected.

Though the environmental movement has gained at least a toehold for a precautionary approach to powerful new technologies, this principle is often disregarded when technical innovations are presented as medical advances. And that is a move that the biotechnology industry and its supporters have mastered. Their claims about the future of human genetic technologies are nothing if not ambitious. Revolutions in health care are invoked. Promises of imminent medical miracles proliferate. Technical fixes for global health inequities are proposed and funded. Senior researchers are unembarrassed to suggest that aging, even death, can be overcome through biotechnological engineering.

Reproductive Genetic Technology

The most troubling of the human biotechnologies are those that involve reproduction. Currently, the procedure known as preimplantation genetic diagnosis (PGD) allows the screening and selecting of embryos on the basis of sex and other traits. Many feminists and disability rights advocates are deeply uneasy about this practice. But for some enthusiasts, such crude forms of selection are just the beginning. More than a few observers predict that in vitro embryos will one day be manipulated and modified rather than merely screened and selected. They point out that the genetic technologies now being used routinely to alter mammalian species, if applied to humans, would permit the "redesign" of the traits of future children.

Some proponents of inheritable genetic modification (IGM) predict that within a generation "enhanced" babies will be born with increased resistance to diseases, optimized height and weight, and increased intelligence. Farther off, but within the lifetimes of today's children, they foresee the ability to adjust personality, design new bodily forms, extend life expectancy, and endow hyper-intelligence.

A New Eugenics

Eagerness to provide parents with the technical means to redesign their future offspring is often coupled with a larger social vision. Advocates of IGM point out that manipulating the genetic makeup of future generations amounts to "seizing control of human evolution." They correctly observe that coupling the techniques of inheritable genetic modification with existing social and market dynamics could trigger a self-reinforcing spiral of eugenic engineering, perhaps culminating in the abandonment of our common biological identity as human beings. Some anticipate a "post-human" future, called into existence through consumer choices in a market-based eugenics, and the subsequent emergence of "genetic castes."

Is such a future likely? Hopefully, scenarios like these will remain beyond technical reach. Notwithstanding the flesh-and-blood accomplishments of today's genetic scientists—glow-in-the-dark rabbits, goats that lactate spider silk, and the like—modified genes and artificial chromosomes may never work reliably. Transgenic designer babies may be too ridden with unpredictability or malfunction to ever become a popular option.

It is at this historical moment that a small U.S.-based nongovernmental organization [NGO] has written and proffered the Genetic Bill of Rights.

But both the trajectory of human biotechnology and the growing ideological influence of high-biotech libertarian futurism counsel that we take these visions seriously. After all, their purveyors are not limited to the marginal "cowboy cloners" and others on the far shore of credibility. Also among those who eagerly anticipate a post-human future are congeries of biomedical researchers, biotech entrepreneurs, bioethicists, and other scholars. A disturbing number of them are respected figures working at prestigious institutions and wielding significant cultural influence. Also disquieting is the near silence of their scientific colleagues. Many of them must have qualms about the use of biotechnology in the service of a new eugenics, but few have publicly registered concern.

The Genetic Bill of Rights

It is at this historical moment that a small U.S.-based nongovernmental organization [NGO] has written and proffered the Genetic Bill of Rights. Like other declarations of rights, this one makes bold claims about the social conditions that characterize our world, and about those that should. The Genetic Bill of Rights asserts the profound consequentiality of new knowledge in the genetic sciences and new techniques of biological manipulation, and of the legal and commercial contexts in which they are being developed and deployed. And it asserts the urgency of establishing a broad consensus about how the new knowledge and technologies should be governed.

In a landmark article titled "Protecting the Endangered Human: Toward an International Treaty Prohibiting Cloning and Inheritable Alterations," published in the *American Journal of Law & Medicine*, George Annas, Lori Andrews, and Rosario Isasi argue that the human condition of belonging to a single biological species is "central to the meaning and enforcement of human rights." Because reproductive cloning and inheritable genetic modification "can alter the essence of humanity itself," they write, these techniques "threaten to change the foundation of human rights." For this reason, the authors say, "cloning and inheritable genetic modification can be seen as crimes against humanity of a unique sort."

In many parts of the world outside the United States, the technologies of human genetic redesign are commonly and comfortably viewed through the lens of human rights. These procedures would be easily and widely understood as violations of what the Genetic Bill of Rights calls "the right to have been conceived, gestated, and born without genetic manipulation." Especially in light of the fact that neither reproductive cloning nor inheritable genetic modification has yet been applied to human beings, the strength of the sentiment for national and international bans on them is striking.

Some dozens of countries have already passed such bans, and several important multilateral instruments address these technologies under the rubric of human rights. The Council of Europe, for example, prohibits both inheritable genetic modification and human reproductive cloning in its Convention on Human Rights and Biomedicine, which was opened for signatures in 1997 after several years of negotiations and preparations. Similarly, UNESCO's [United Nations Educational, Scientific and Cultural Organization] Universal Declaration on the Human Genome and Human Rights, though not a legally binding document, forbids the production of cloned human beings, and says that inheritable genetic modification "could be contrary to human dignity."

Rights in the United States

In the United States, the claim of a right "to have been conceived, gestated, and born without genetic manipulation" resonates less strongly. We tend to think of "rights," including "human rights," as shielding individuals from the coercive power of the state. However, today commercial entities often have as much control over individuals' life choices and destinies as do governments. If the biotechnology and assisted reproduction industries were to decide to develop "genetic enhancement" procedures and market them to prospective parents, the pressures to "provide the best start in life for your child" would be considerable. Health insurance companies would likely weigh in. Coercion of parents need not necessarily be enforced by governmental authority to be effective. And the children in question, of course, would have no protection—unless we establish that freedom from genetic manipulation is indeed a human right.

We in the United States often focus so sharply on individual rights and liberties that we blur our perception of the social conditions that foster or block their enjoyment.

In the individualist culture of the United States, rights are usually meant first and foremost to protect and enlarge individual liberties. The discourse of human rights, by contrast, implies as well the imperative of safeguarding the collective conditions in which people and communities can flourish. In the United States, we tend also to characterize rights as applying to us as autonomous beings who choose our own values and chart our own lives, rather than as people unavoidably situated in complex and overlapping relationships with each other. As autonomous individuals, we go it alone. As social beings necessarily dependent on each other in myriad fashion, we are obligated to struggle together toward shared understandings about the kind of world we want to build.

Finally, we in the United States often focus so sharply on individual rights and liberties that we blur our perception of the social conditions that foster or block their enjoyment. We sometimes forget, in other words, that rights are necessarily embedded in relations of power. But championing rights in the abstract, without considering the political and social inequities with which we live, can undermine our commitments to social justice and solidarity, and to the democratic principle that we can and ought to participate in decisions about the basic conditions of our polity and collective life.

Individual Liberty and Social Justice

In her investigation of the tension between individual liberty and social justice as it pertains to reproductive rights and racial equality, legal scholar Dorothy Roberts asserts that the "dominant view of liberty reserves most of its protection only for the most privileged members of society." By contrast, she argues that "reproductive freedom is a matter of social justice," and that "procreation's special status stems as much from its role in social structure and political relations as from its meaning to individuals." She is appalled that advocates of the new eugenics can present themselves as champions of freedom even as they "dismiss the possibility that genetic enhancement might exacerbate race and class disparities."

Liberties and rights, no matter how loudly they are proclaimed to be "self-evident," are always the results of social arrangements, often painfully arrived at, on matters of common concern. Most nations of the world have now abolished slavery. Many have criminalized marital rape and outlawed the selling and abuse of children. These are examples of widely accepted limits on practices once construed as rights.

In practice, the two conceptualizations of rights—call them the individual-choice-and-autonomy model and the social-justice-and-negotiation model—often coexist in the same policy formulation. For example, the right not to be enslaved protects individuals from being subjected to involuntary servitude, yet the same right also bespeaks a socially negotiated—albeit once hotly contested—agreement that a world in which some have the power to enslave others is not a world in which we wish to live.

The Right to Be Free of Genetic Manipulation

How does all this apply to the proposed "right to have been conceived, gestated, and born without genetic manipulation"? Advocates of market-based eugenics, appealing to the widely accepted consumer-oriented norms of our society, and to the very high value it places on individual liberty, scientific freedom, and technological advance, argue that people have the right to select the traits of their future children. Often they present this as an extension of reproductive choice and "procreative liberty."

These assertions can be countered even from within the individual-choice-and-autonomy model of rights. Experience with cloned and transgenic animals demonstrates that such procedures would carry enormous risks for both the cloned or genetically modified child and for the child's mother. As developmental biologist Stuart Newman points out, "No amount of data from laboratory animals will make the first human trials anything but experimental." And since there is little medical justification for such procedures, they would represent a clear-cut case of unethical human experimentation.

Furthermore, it would be impossible to obtain what bioethicists call "informed consent" from the person to be cloned or modified, since the procedure would have to be carried out well before birth. And reproductive cloning and inheritable genetic modification would arguably compromise the autonomy of the cloned or modified person, since his or her life would have been controlled in an unprecedented manner by the parents, fertility doctors, and biotech companies involved.

The social-justice-and-negotiation model of rights provides additional support for the proposed right to be born free of genetic manipulation. It attends with care to the likelihood that the commercial development of reproductive cloning and IGM would exacerbate existing inequalities and create new forms of discrimination and inequality. It heeds the dangers of granting novel forms of control over individuals' lives, and over the genetic legacy of the human species, to any public or private entity.

The Genetic Bill of Rights, and the "right to have been conceived, gestated, and born without genetic manipulation" that it contains, is a statement of political will and moral intelligence. In an era that has witnessed dire consequences of technological grandiosity, it calls for extending the precautionary principle to our own biology. In an age of runaway elitism, it calls for affirming our common humanity as a minimal but crucial condition of solidarity and mutuality. In the face of efforts to inscribe inequality into the human genome, it insists that—like it or not—we're all in this together.

Regulation of Reproduction Will Be Necessary to Limit Genetic Enhancement

Samuel Berger

Samuel Berger is a law student and former special assistant to the senior fellows at the Center for American Progress, a progressive think tank.

The potential for new biotechnologies to have far-reaching societal consequences presents a novel challenge to the progressive belief that people have an unrestricted right to make any and all of their own reproductive choices. Previous scientific advances such as the sonogram have altered the abortion debate by affecting public opinion about the moral status of the fetus; but these earlier technologies have not substantially weakened the support among progressives for unrestricted reproductive choice. That soon may change.

Self-Regarding Acts

Current technologies such as preimplantation genetic diagnosis [PGD] and sperm sorting—and possible future technologies such as cloning and germ line modification—will enable parents to make decisions that greatly affect gender balance, disease burdens, genetic diversity and the genes of humans themselves. In order to address these new possibilities adequately, we will need to find a way to regulate some choices while maintaining existing reproductive freedoms.

The shifting parameters of reproductive choice will oblige Americans of all political persuasions—but above all progressives—to revisit some of our most dearly held tenets. Support for reproductive choice is grounded in the notion that the

Samuel Berger, "A Challenge to Progressives on Choice," *The Nation*, July 18, 2007. www.thenation.com. Reproduced by permission.

choices themselves are private matters that are the individual's alone. In *On Liberty*, for example, a classic foundational work of liberal political theory, John Stuart Mill outlined two types of actions: self-regarding acts, which largely affect only the individuals carrying them out, and other-regarding acts, which substantially affect people in addition to the acting individual. Mill argued that while regulation or prohibition was appropriate for other-regarding acts, it was not for self-regarding acts.

Americans have largely adopted this distinction, regulating choices only when they affect others in the larger community. Nowhere is this clearer than in the debate around abortion, where the fundamental question is whether a person thinks the choice affects others. The extent to which reproductive choices are self-regarding or other-regarding—and thus the extent to which they should be regulated—revolves around one's view of the moral status of the embryo or fetus.

Most progressives consider abortion and other reproductive choices self-regarding acts, because the fetus or embryo is not seen as a separate person with equal and competing interests. As NARAL Pro-Choice America describes them, reproductive choices should not be regulated, because they are private decisions women make with "their families, their physicians, and their faith."

The Increase in Reproductive Technologies

Biotechnological innovations, however, are quickly shifting certain reproductive decisions from matters of private choice to ones of public concern, regardless of the moral status of fetuses and embryos. Parents in the twenty-first century will have the ability to control the genetic makeup of their children in ways that were unthinkable fifty years ago. The choices they make will thus significantly affect the structure of society. As progressives, we must acknowledge the new challenges posed by these reproductive technologies and, when necessary, craft policies to limit their potentially harmful impact.

Already, people undergoing in vitro fertilization (IVF) can use preimplantation genetic diagnosis to choose which embryos are implanted based on their genetics, screening potential embryos for debilitating diseases or choosing "savior siblings," who have the genetic makeup necessary to be compatible donors for a sick child. They can also use PGD to select the sex of their child, or use a less effective technique that involves sorting the sperm before artificial insemination or IVF.

Through IVF, future parents will theoretically be able to select embryos for other characteristics such as height or hair color. While many assisted reproductive technologies including PGD are currently expensive and infrequently used, improvements will likely reduce expense and increase demand as parents can have more control for less cost.

Which conditions are acceptable to screen for, as well as whether and how screening should be encouraged, are questions that must be answered collectively.

The increasing use of PGD to choose children's characteristics could greatly affect disease rates in society, as well as our conception of responsibility for those diseases. Currently, there is significant support for using the procedure to prevent implanting embryos with early onset, life-threatening diseases. But what about using it to choose children with or without a less debilitating condition?

The Effects of Individual Reproductive Choices

Fertility clinics currently allow parents to screen embryos for Down syndrome; a British couple is screening their embryo for early-onset Alzheimer's [disease]; and a London hospital has proposed discarding male embryos to prevent autism, which is more prevalent among males, in at-risk families.

Some parents with deafness or dwarfism have suggested that they want to purposefully select children with a similar condition.

Individual choices could thus have a huge effect on the structure of our health care system, as well as the market for cures—there would be little incentive for pharmaceutical companies to develop drugs to treat conditions all but eliminated by PGD, particularly since wealthier families will likely be the first to have widespread access to this expensive technology. And these choices could also affect the availability of services for children with these disabilities or illnesses. Which conditions are acceptable to screen for, as well as whether and how screening should be encouraged, are questions that must be answered collectively.

PGD and sperm sorting also offer the opportunity for easy and efficient sex selection of children. Results of a recent survey suggest that 42 percent of U.S. fertility clinics have already used PGD to do so for nonmedical reasons. While these actions may seem harmless, they have the potential to lead to dangerous gender imbalances: An overabundance of either males or females could have tremendous effects on marriage, sex-trafficking, crime rates and stability.

People able to afford these expensive procedures will be able to select for more genetically advantaged children, potentially allowing the rich to get genetically richer.

Countries such as India and China already have significant imbalances created through abortion and infanticide, and increased access to ultrasound in China has further exacerbated the imbalance. PGD and sperm sorting will make the process easier and more socially acceptable because parents can make the decision to select a specific sex before becoming pregnant.

The Future of PGD

Future use of PGD, however, may even allow parents to select for more specific traits such as height, hair color or body type as parents seek to have the "perfect child." These choices could dangerously narrow the gene pool—with attendant risks of increased susceptibility to disease or unintended amplification of debilitating genes.

There could also be wide-reaching cultural, sociological and political effects from a drastically less diverse population including increased pressure to conform to cultural, and eventually genetic, norms and decreased acceptance of differences among people. The use of these technologies could also dangerously exacerbate existing inequalities. People able to afford these expensive procedures will be able to select for more genetically advantaged children, potentially allowing the rich to get genetically richer, while the poor do not.

As difficult as breaking the cycle of poverty is today as the result of environmental factors, imagine having a society with exaggerated differences in physical and intellectual abilities as well as disease susceptibilities. And citizens with increased resistance to disease, or fewer genetic risk factors, may be loath to pay into shared-risk programs with a clientele of less "genetically fit" people. The potential for discrimination, the breakdown of social safety nets, and entrenched inequality would be immense.

Genetic Modification and Cloning

The ability to select children's traits through PGD, however, is only the tip of the iceberg. Far more worrisome is the future potential to alter the genetic makeup of children themselves through techniques such as germ line modification—the genetic modification of human germ cells (sperm, eggs, or embryos) resulting in inheritable changes. Germ line modification is supported by some groups as a matter of reproductive choice—even though germ line modification, unlike other forms of genetic enhancement, would not only change the genetic structure of a child according to its parents' specifications but would cause those altered genes to be passed on to the child's offspring.

Along with many of the risks associated with PGD, germ line modification technology could potentially produce new beings that are not even entirely human, but rather a combination of human and nonhuman genetic material. Genetically altered humans would almost certainly commingle with the rest of society, thereby affecting the offspring of other individuals and leading to new and unexpected genetic combinations. Choosing when to start a family is undoubtedly a personal matter, but choosing the future genetic makeup of the human race affects us all.

Human cloning technology presents similar problems for society, though they are likely to be less prevalent. Creating a child who is almost an exact genetic duplicate of someone else could affect disease burdens and, to a lesser extent, genetic diversity, as well as fundamentally alter the nature of human reproduction from sexual to asexual. While no scientists are advocating this practice, liberal intellectual Laurence Tribe cautions against banning reproductive cloning because of "concern [about] the very decision to use the law to condemn and then outlaw patterns of human reproduction." He worries that it might "lend credence to strikingly similar objections to surrogate motherhood or gay marriage and gay adoption."

The most reasonable solution is regulation.

Although no regulation of human reproduction should be undertaken lightly, there are compelling reasons to ban reproductive cloning, should the technology become available including problems related to the safety and efficacy of the process, as well as ethical concerns. The irrevocable change that reproductive cloning could bring to the family structure, particularly the relationship between parent and child, makes it hard to argue that such drastic changes should be left solely to individual decision and not be examined by society collectively.

The Need for Regulation

So what is the appropriate response to these current and future issues? The most reasonable solution is regulation. Progressives are understandably wary of regulating anything related to reproductive decision making. But an unregulated fertility industry is even more unappealing. Certain unregulated individual reproductive choices in a market system could easily lead to undesirable societal outcomes, particularly because individuals would be unlikely to sacrifice perceived benefits to their children for the seemingly abstract concept of the common good.

The current state of self-regulation of US fertility clinics, which has been likened to the Wild West, demonstrates that voluntary professional guidelines will not be enough. And clearly Congress does not have the scientific expertise to address each of these issues individually in a timely or effective manner. The courts would prove an equally awkward and ill-suited means of dealing with these problems, particularly in the absence of relevant laws.

One promising idea, outlined by Francis Fukuyama and Franco Furger in *Beyond Bioethics: A Proposal for Modernizing the Regulation of Human Biotechnologies*, is for the government to create a new regulatory body specifically for reproductive technologies. Although the authors remain focused on the well-being of the particular individuals involved and not the larger effects on society, the proposal is not wedded to specific regulatory outcomes.

Other countries have already established regulatory authorities for some reproductive technologies, with no adverse consequences for access to abortion and contraception. Britain created the Human Fertilisation and Embryology Authority in 1990 to regulate fertility clinics, embryo research, and the storage of embryos and gametes. Canada is in the process of creating Assisted Human Reproduction Canada, which was established in 2006 to oversee assisted human reproduction. Britain regulates the use of PGD, restricting its use to certain diseases, and Canada will regulate the process as well. Both Britain and Canada currently prohibit reproductive cloning and germ line modification, which are legal in the United States.

Of course, there are many questions that must be answered about such a regulatory agency in the United States, including its composition, scope and powers. But despite legitimate concerns that such an agency should not unduly constrain reproductive rights, some regulation of certain current and potential reproductive technologies is needed. A regulatory body serves little purpose, however, without a theoretical framework to inform it.

In order to maintain existing protections for reproductive choices we view as self-regarding and personal, we need to delineate clearly which of them require oversight and which do not.

Drawing the Line

Progressives, then, will need a new way to distinguish what reproductive technologies and practices should be regulated. While there is no clear answer, there are a number of possibilities. Progressives could distinguish biotechnologies based on their likely effect on society—ones that will have little or no foreseeable negative effect would remain unregulated. We could also consider regulating biotechnologies based on the best interests of the potential child, assuming we could determine them.

Alternatively, a distinction could be made between reproductive decisions to have a child and those regarding the genetic makeup of that child. We also might regulate technological uses that are inherently discriminatory or likely to affect disproportionately and adversely some discrete and insular minorities. Or a line could be drawn between regulating the use of certain technologies and regulating individual choices themselves.

All of these suggestions have strengths and weaknesses, including the difficulty in determining how biotechnologies should be classified and the potential for regulation to be too broad or too narrow. What is important, however, is that progressives start debating the merits of these and other potential conceptual frameworks.

Whether we like it or not, some reproductive decisions are becoming matters of societal interest, and we need to be clear on where we think society should draw the line. In order to maintain existing protections for reproductive choices we view as self-regarding and personal, we need to delineate clearly which of them require oversight and which do not.

CHAPTER 4

Should Genes Be Available for Patent?

Overview: Gene Patents

U.S. Department of Energy Office of Science

The U.S. Department of Energy Office of Science is the largest supporter of basic research in the physical sciences in the United States.

The patentability of inventions under U.S. law is determined by the [U.S.] Patent and Trademark Office (USPTO) in the Department of Commerce. A patent application is judged on four criteria. The invention must be "useful" in a practical sense (the inventor must identify some useful purpose for it), "novel" (i.e., not known or used before the filing), and "nonobvious" (i.e., not an improvement easily made by someone trained in the relevant area). The invention also must be described in sufficient detail to enable one skilled in the field to use it for the stated purpose (sometimes called the "enablement" criterion).

Biotechnology Patents

In general, raw products of nature are not patentable. DNA products usually become patentable when they have been isolated, purified, or modified to produce a unique form not found in nature.

The USPTO has 3 years to issue a patent. In Europe, the time frame is 18 months. The USPTO is adopting a similar system. Patents are good for 20 years from filing date.

In the United States, patent priority is based on the "first to invent" principle: Whoever made the invention first (and can prove it) is awarded property rights for the 20-year period. Inventors have a one-year grace period to file after

"Genetics and Patenting," U.S. Department of Energy Office of Science, September 16, 2008.

they publish. All other countries except the Philippines, however, follow a "first inventor to file" rule in establishing priority when granting patents.

Many biotech patents have been applied for as provisional patents. This means that persons or companies filing the provisional patent application have up to one year to file their actual patent claim. The provisional patent must contain a written description of said invention and the names of the inventors. This one-year grace period does not count as one of the 20 years that the patent is issued for.

When a biotechnology patent involving an altered product of nature is issued, the patent holder is required to deposit a sample of the new invention into one of the 26 worldwide culture depositories. Most DNA-related patents are issued by the USPTO, the European Patent Office, or the Japan Patent Office.

Currently over three million genome-related patent applications have been filed. U.S. patent applications are confidential until a patent is issued, so determining which sequences are the subject of patent applications is impossible. Those who use sequences from public databases today risk facing a future injunction if those sequences turn out to be patented by a private company on the basis of previously filed patent applications.

In terms of genetics, inventors must

1. identify novel genetic sequences,

2. specify the sequence's product,

3. specify how the product functions in nature—its use, and

4. enable one skilled in the field to use the sequence for its stated purpose.

Patents for Gene Fragments

USPTO has issued a few patents for gene fragments. Full sequence and function often are not known for gene fragments. On pending applications, their utility has been identified by such vague definitions as providing scientific probes to help find a gene or another EST [expressed sequence tag] or to help map a chromosome. Questions have arisen over the issue of when, from discovery to development into useful products, exclusive rights to genes could be claimed.

The 300- to 500-base gene fragments, called expressed sequence tags [ESTs], represent only 10% to 30% of the average cDNA [complementary DNA], and the genomic genes are often 10 to 20 times larger than the cDNA. A cDNA molecule is a laboratory-made version of a gene that contains only its information-rich (exon) regions; these molecules provide a way for genome researchers to fast-forward through the genome to biologically important areas. The original chromosomal locations and biological functions of the full genes identified by ESTs are unknown in most cases.

A Controversy

Patent applications for such gene fragments have sparked controversy among scientists, many of whom have urged the USPTO not to grant broad patents in this early stage of human genome research to applicants who have neither characterized the genes nor determined their functions and uses.

The patenting of gene fragments is controversial.

In December 1999, the USPTO issued stiffer interim guidelines (made final in January 2001) stating that more usefulness—specifically how the product functions in nature—must now be shown before gene fragments are considered patentable. The new rules call for "specific and substantial utility that is credible," but some still feel the rules are too lax.

The patenting of gene fragments is controversial. Some say that patenting such discoveries is inappropriate because the effort to find any given EST is small compared with the work of isolating and characterizing a gene and gene product, finding out what it does, and developing a commercial product. They feel that allowing holders of such "gatekeeper" patents to exercise undue control over the commercial fruits of genome research would be unfair. Similarly, allowing multiple patents on different parts of the same genome sequence—say on a gene fragment, the gene, and the protein—adds undue costs to the researcher who wants to examine the sequence. Not only does the researcher have to pay each patent holder via licensing for the opportunity to study the sequence, he also has to pay his own staff to research the different patents and determine which are applicable to the area of the genome he wants to study.

Patents for Single Nucleotide Polymorphisms

Single nucleotide polymorphisms (SNPs) are DNA sequence variations that occur when a single nucleotide (A, T, C, or G) in the genome sequence is altered. For example a SNP might change the DNA sequence AAGGCTAA to ATGGCTAA. SNPs occur every 100 to 1,000 bases along the 3-billion-base human genome. SNPs can occur in both coding (gene) and noncoding regions of the genome. Many SNPs have no effect on cell function, but scientists believe others could predispose people to disease or influence their response to a drug.

Variations in DNA sequence can have a major impact on how humans respond to disease; environmental insults such as bacteria, viruses, toxins, and chemicals; and drugs and other therapies. This makes SNPs of great value for biomedical research and for developing pharmaceutical products or medical diagnostics. Scientists believe SNP maps will help them identify the multiple genes associated with such complex diseases as cancer, diabetes, vascular disease, and some forms of mental illness. These associations are difficult to establish with conventional gene-hunting methods because a single altered gene may make only a small contribution to the disease.

As disease genes are found, complementary gene tests are developed to screen for the gene in humans who suspect they may be at risk for developing the disease.

In April 1999, ten large pharmaceutical companies and the U.K. Wellcome Trust philanthropy announced the establishment of a nonprofit foundation to find and map 300,000 common SNPs (they found 1.8 million). Their goal was to generate a widely accepted, high-quality, extensive, publicly available map using SNPs as markers evenly distributed throughout the human genome. The consortium planned to patent all the SNPs found but to enforce the patents only to prevent others from patenting the same information. Information found by the consortium is freely available.

Patents for Gene Tests and Proteins

As disease genes are found, complementary gene tests are developed to screen for the gene in humans who suspect they may be at risk for developing the disease. These tests are usually patented and licensed by the owners of the disease gene patent. Royalties are due the patent holder each time the tests are administered, and only licensed entities can conduct the tests.

Proteins do the work of the cell. A complete set of genetic information is contained in each cell. This information provides a specific set of instructions to the body. The body carries out these instructions via proteins. Genes encode proteins.

All living organisms are composed largely of proteins, which have three main cellular functions: to provide cell structure and be involved in cell signaling and cell communication functions. Enzymes are proteins.

Patents for stem cells from monkeys and other organisms already have been issued.

Proteins are important to researchers because they are the links between genes and pharmaceutical development. They indicate which genes are expressed or are being used. Important for understanding gene function, proteins also have unique shapes or structures. Understanding these structures, and how potential pharmaceuticals will bind to them, is a key element in drug design.

The Patenting of Stem Cells

Therapeutic cloning, also called "embryo cloning" or "cloning for biomedical research," is the production of human embryos for use in research. The goal of this process is not to create cloned human beings but rather to harvest stem cells that can be used to study human development and treat disease. Stem cells are important to biomedical researchers because they can be used to generate virtually any type of specialized cell in the human body. . . .

Cell lines and genetically modified single-cell organisms are considered patentable material. One of the earliest cases involving the patentability of single-cell organisms was *Diamond v. Chakrabarty* in 1980, in which the Supreme Court ruled that genetically modified bacteria were patentable.

Patents for stem cells from monkeys and other organisms already have been issued. Therefore, based on past court rulings, human embryonic stem cells are technically patentable. A lot of social and legal controversy has developed in response to the potential patentability of human stem cells. A major concern is that patents for human stem cells and human cloning techniques violate the principle against the ownership of human beings. In the U.S. patent system, patents are granted based on existing technical patent criteria. Ethical concerns have not influenced this process in the past, but, the stem cell debate may change this. It will be interesting to see how patent law regarding stem cell research will play out.

The Justification for Patents

Research scientists who work in public institutions often are troubled by the concept of intellectual property because their norms tell them that science will advance more rapidly if researchers enjoy free access to knowledge. By contrast, the law of intellectual property rests on an assumption that, without exclusive rights, no one will be willing to invest in research and development (R&D).

Patenting provides a strategy for protecting inventions without secrecy. A patent grants the right to exclude others from making, using, and selling the invention for a limited term, 20 years from application filing date in most of the world. To get a patent, an inventor must disclose the invention fully so as to enable others to make and use it. Within the realm of industrial research, the patent system promotes more disclosure than would occur if secrecy were the only means of excluding competitors. This is less clear in the case of public-sector research, which typically is published with or without patent protection.

The argument for patenting public-sector inventions is a variation on the standard justification for patents in commercial settings. The argument is that post-invention development costs typically far exceed pre-invention research outlays, and firms are unwilling to make this substantial investment without protection from competition. Patents thus facilitate transfer of technology to the private sector by providing exclusive rights to preserve the profit incentives of innovating firms.

Patents are generally considered to be very positive. In the case of genetic patenting, it is the scope and number of claims that has generated controversy.

Gene Patents Work the Way Patents Are Supposed to Work

John E. Calfee

John E. Calfee is a resident scholar at the American Enterprise Institute for Public Policy Research, an organization dedicated to research and education on issues of government, politics, economics, and social welfare.

The *New York Times* ran a story on May 13 [2009] about a lawsuit brought by a breast cancer patient and several co-plaintiffs against Myriad Genetics, a biotech firm that owns a patent to a diagnostic test for the BRCA1 and BRCA2 genes (not mentioned by name in the story), which are involved in a particularly dangerous form of breast and ovarian cancer. These kinds of cancers rarely respond to targeted biotech treatments such as Herceptin, so the BRCA test can help inform treatment and encourage use of preventive measures. The lawsuit apparently originated from the lead plaintiff's discovery that this rather expensive test (about $3,000) is offered only by Myriad and must be performed on their premises in Salt Lake City, Utah, because Myriad owns not only a patent for the test but also for the BRCA genes themselves. The plaintiffs think the U.S. Patent and Trademark Office (PTO) grievously erred when it granted these patents and, in fact, has erred in granting any gene patents at all. One of the academic researchers and co-plaintiffs was quoted to the effect that gene patents like this one not only increase medical costs but also impede academic research.

John E. Calfee, "Decoding the Use of Gene Patents," *American*, May 15, 2009. Reproduced with the permission of the American Enterprise Institute for Public Policy Research, Washington, DC.

Two Complaints About Gene Patents

The *Times* story, which I suspect was better balanced than many of the news stories soon to follow, noted that a 2006 report from the National Academy of Sciences [NAS] found little evidence that gene patents had adversely affected research. As you might expect, there is more to this story, although the bottom line is consistent with the academy's report rather than with the tenor of the *Times* article as a whole. Human genes can be patented, but not simply by decoding a snippet of DNA and sending a sequence of the letters A, G, C, and T to the PTO. You have to isolate and purify the gene segment in a way that does not occur in nature, and you have to establish some sort of concrete use—"utility" is the standard word—in order to satisfy PTO standards. Gene patents were extremely controversial when the PTO started awarding them. The PTO prevailed against considerable academic and political opposition, however, and eventually the European Union followed suit. A little-appreciated part of this story is that a lot of these patents have been filed not by private firms but by universities on behalf of their researchers. As it happens, some of the BRCA patents are actually co-owned by Myriad's neighbor, the University of Utah.

Like most economists I support the granting of patents and their consequent pricing power as a tool to foster innovation.

There are really two complaints about gene patents. One is that when a gene patent gives a seller a monopoly over a product, that product will be sold at monopoly prices, which can be much higher than the competitive price—and moreover, as the plaintiff in the gene patent litigation noticed, that single seller can restrict how a diagnostic is used in addition to how it is priced. Of course, that is what we expect with patented products, and like most economists I support the granting of patents and their consequent pricing power as a tool to foster innovation.

There is another possible problem with gene patents, however: They could get in the way of research. As an academic plaintiff noted in the *Times* story, research often involves sifting through all sorts of genetic details including ones that happen to have been patented by someone else. One potentially disastrous scenario is a "patent thicket" in which research is hemmed in by the possibility of bumping into all sorts of patents such as those the researcher never knew existed. Hundreds or thousands of patent infringement suits could ensue with their legendary costs and delay. In theory, elaborate patent pools could forestall this problem but that would be costly too, in terms of patent searches and multiparty negotiations.

There is much to be said for broad licensing of gene patents and diagnostics based upon them.

Patents and Research

A number of interested parties including the National Academy of Sciences sought to explore these problems. On the whole, the news is very good. The NAS has twice commissioned surveys led by John Walsh, a well-qualified expert, and both times, little evidence emerged that research laboratories were hemmed in by gene patents (summarized in the same NAS report cited earlier). It turns out that researchers seldom worry about what is patented and what is not. Moreover, litigation has been amazingly rare. That was documented in a 2008 article in *Science* magazine, which found that only six lawsuits had been filed in connection with gene-patented diagnostics and all had been dismissed or settled, apparently with negligible impact on scholarly research. Just two months ago [March 2009], the journal *Nature*, Britain's version of *Sci-*

ence (or the other way around, the Brits could justifiably claim), published two articles and an editorial on gene patents. The title of one of those articles, "The Phantom Menace of Gene Patents" is a pretty good summary of the latest findings. The other article [by Robert Cook-Deegan, Subhashini Chandrasekharan, and Misha Angrist] concluded that "prices of patented and exclusively licensed tests are not dramatically or consistently higher than those of tests without a monopoly"—a very different scenario from that suggested by the Myriad lawsuit. An accompanying editorial, which emphasized academic gene patenting and was entitled "Property Rights," concluded that "dire predictions that patents will cripple genetics research should be viewed with skepticism on both sides of the Atlantic."

This is not to say there have been no problems at all. But the PTO has resisted parties' over-reaching, such as by attempting to file thousands of gene patents simultaneously with scant attention to "utility." And there is much to be said for broad licensing of gene patents and diagnostics based upon them. On the whole, though, gene patents are turning out to work more or less the way patents are supposed to work and have been working for a couple of centuries and more. The research process, and ultimately patients, are the beneficiaries.

Gene Patents Have Not Had a Negative Effect on Research

E. Jonathan Soderstrom

E. Jonathan Soderstrom is managing director of the Yale University Office of Cooperative Research, which oversees patenting and licensing activities.

Scholars have recently argued that patents may impose significant costs upon noncommercial biomedical research. [Michael] Heller and [Rebecca] Eisenberg suggest that the patenting of a broad range of the inputs that researchers need to do their work may give rise to an "anti-commons" or "patent thicket" that may make the acquisition of licenses and other rights too burdensome to permit the pursuit of what should otherwise be scientifically and socially worthwhile research. [Robert] Merges and [Richard] Nelson and [Suzanne] Scotchmer highlight the related possibility that, in some fields of technology, the assertion of patents on only one or two key upstream, foundational discoveries may significantly restrict follow-on research. A further concern is that the prospect of realizing financial gain from upstream research may make researchers reluctant to share information or research materials with one another, thereby impeding the realization of research efficiencies and complementarities. Similarly, researchers may be trading away rights to conduct future research or to freely disseminate their discoveries in exchange for current access to research inputs or financial support. Finally, prospective financial gains from the exploitation of intellectual property may induce researchers to choose research projects on the basis of commercial potential rather than scientific merit.

E. Jonathan Soderstrom, "Hearing on Stifling or Stimulating—The Role of Gene Patents in Research and Genetic Testing," House Committee on the Judiciary, Subcommittee on Courts, the Internet, and Intellectual Property Web site: judiciary.house.gov/hearings, October 30, 2007.

Anecdotal Evidence

Another aspect of the debate about whether intellectual property fosters or hinders biomedical research relates to the "research tools," which are the ideas, data, materials or methods used to conduct research. Many such materials and methods are disclosed or claimed in DNA patents. Among DNA patents, there is particular concern about the subset of gene patents and their relevance to research tools because genes are not only inputs to developing genetic tests and therapeutic proteins, and thus directly relevant to medically important products and services, but also are crucially important tools for ongoing research. Concern over the impact of patenting and licensing on biomedical research has grown since the Court of Appeals for the Federal Circuit's 2002 *Madey v. Duke* decision, which visibly affirmed the absence of any research exemption shielding universities from patent infringement liability. Patent claims based on DNA sequences can be infringed by research activities that entail making or using the claimed sequence, not just by selling products or services.

The licensing of DNA patents at US academic institutions has not led to the decline in academic cooperation and technology transfer that many observers have feared.

Without diminishing the importance of these potential concerns, it should be pointed out that the evidence offered to support these contentions is primarily anecdotal. Although these isolated instances have received significant attention, there is no evidence that widespread assertion of patent rights on genes has significantly hampered biomedical research. Contrary to these prevailing beliefs, findings from a recent survey of 414 biomedical researchers in universities, government, and nonprofit institutions offer little empirical basis for claims that restricted access to intellectual property is currently impeding academic biomedical research. The authors noted that, although common, patents in this field are not typically used to restrict access to the knowledge and tangible materials that biomedical scientists require.

The authors cite a number of reasons, including the fact that firms generally do not threaten infringement litigation against academic research institutions (a *de facto* research exemption), in part because such academic use may improve their invention, because they wish to maintain good will and to ensure access to future academic inventions, and also because the damages are likely to be very small. According to the authors:

> "Our research thus suggests that 'law on the books' need not be the same as 'law in action' if the law on the books contravenes a community's norms and interests."

A Survey of Academic Institutions

These findings are consistent with another recent major survey of 19 of the 30 US universities with the largest number of DNA patents. Their results showed that the licensing of DNA patents at US academic institutions has not led to the decline in academic cooperation and technology transfer that many observers have feared. In fact, based on responses, the study demonstrated that in most cases the licensing behavior of universities allows for collaboration and sharing of DNA-based inventions among academic institutions.

The study investigated the patenting and licensing behavior for four main types of DNA-based inventions:

- DNA sequences that encode therapeutic proteins

- DNA sequences that are phenotypic markers only

- DNA sequences comprising genes encoding drug targets

- DNA discoveries or inventions representing research tools

The authors discovered that most universities base their decisions to patent and strategies for commercializing the invention on a determination of the level of protection necessary to induce an interested company into investing in the further development, testing, manufacture, marketing and sale of a product embodying the technology. Thus, in the case of a fully sequenced gene that encodes a therapeutic protein, where the utility and the development risks are both generally acknowledged to be high, survey respondents generally agreed that they would patent and license such inventions exclusively. However, in the case where the gene encoded is simply a target for drug discovery, few would consider even patenting such a discovery since researchers would be free to screen their compound libraries against the target while the patent application was pending and to use any resulting information without fear on infringement. In addition, it has become commonplace for universities, when licensing their inventions, to reserve the right for their own faculty, as well as researchers at other nonprofit entities, to use the patented invention. The study confirmed that university technology managers take a nuanced approach to patenting and licensing, seeking only enough intellectual property protection to facilitate the commercial development of the invention.

We do not think that gene patents are having a significant negative impact on academic research.

This market sensitivity is also reflected in data on patent trends. The number of DNA patents has shown a fairly dramatic and steady decline since their peak in 2001 (from about 4,500 to around 2,700 in 2005). Patent prosecution, maintenance and management costs that are typically between $20,000 and $30,000 per patent militate against patenting inventions that are unlikely to recover those costs and encourage considerable selectivity in which inventions are patented. . . .

A Balanced Approach

We believe that patent policy, as well as practice, should be guided by the goal of promoting innovation and, in turn, improvements in human welfare. That view drove Yale's interest in helping to draft the "Nine Points" guidelines, which recommend that universities refrain from patenting genomic inventions that will serve primarily as research tools. Yale has long taken a balanced approach to patenting, taking into account the nature of the invention, its relevance to research, and the extent to which patent protection would be necessary to give a commercial partner adequate incentive to develop the product completely. We have taken a similar approach to licensing, especially by insisting upon the right to make the invention available to researchers at Yale and other academic institutions.

We do not think that gene patents are having a significant negative impact on academic research. There have been thoughtful analyses of problems that could arise, and there have been anecdotal reports and two comprehensive studies of this issue . . . that concluded that patents are not slowing the pace of research for several reasons. Universities take a nuanced approach to patenting and they are increasingly making specific provision for research uses of inventions in licenses. There is evidence that a "*de facto* research exemption" exists because companies rarely prosecute academic investigators for research uses that may be infringing.

Yale and other universities have a major stake in ensuring that access to research tools is not compromised (the "Nine Points" document is evidence of that); we also recognize that circumstances may change as the fields of genomics and proteomics continue to advance. I am confident that the scientific community, working with the National Institutes of Health, the Association of University Technology Managers, the Association of American Medical Colleges and others, will continue to monitor whether gene patents are interfering significantly with research.

Gene Patents Create Social and Economic Problems

Christoph Then

Christoph Then is a Greenpeace patent expert. Greenpeace is an independent organization that uses peaceful, direct action and creative communication to draw attention to global environmental problems.

One example of the situations the patenting of genes may lead to was given in *Science* in 1997, under the title "HIV Experts vs. Sequencers in Patent Race." The article describes the discovery of the CCR5 receptor, which caused a great stir in the international scientific community because it plays a major role in the penetration of the AIDS virus into the cell. After many scientists had already looked into the CCR5 receptor and its possible therapeutic implications, they found that Human Genome Sciences had already filed a patent application for the corresponding gene sequence in 1995. Although the patent specification does not even mention a connection with the HIV infection, Human Genome Sciences also claims the rights to this gene in the framework of AIDS research. Jorge Goldstein, the company's attorney, declares: "Whoever is first to patent a DNA sequence—for any use—can lock up subsequent uses."

The Patent Model

A major part of the problem stems from the transfer of patent law from the sphere of chemistry and physics to the living world. In connection with chemistry, so-called product patents can be granted. These cover all properties of the patented substances, independently of whether they are described in

Christoph Then, "The True Cost of Gene Patents: The Economic and Social Consequences of Patenting Genes and Living Organisms," Greenpeace, June 15, 2004. www.greenpeace.org. Reproduced by permission.

the patent specification or not. Only *one single* commercial application needs to be stated in order to receive exclusive control of the substance and *all* its properties. This model was transferred to the genetic code. If one commercial application is described, the patent protects all biological functions of the gene inasmuch as they can be commercially exploited.

Now that the human genome has been decoded and it has become evident that genes usually perform several and often very different functions, this type of patent appears completely inappropriate. Genes now appear to be much more like encoded information than like active chemical substances. The genes that govern the laying of eggs in the threadworm may be responsible for Alzheimer's [disease] in human beings. Genes that cause breast cancer may also play an important role in diseases of the colon or prostate gland. Moreover, under this kind of patent protection, a company that receives a patent connected with a diagnostic procedure also has the rights to the gene if it is used to develop a much more complex therapy or medicine. This monopoly makes no sense either in scientific or in economic terms, since it does far more to hamper research and development than to promote it.

Genes Are Not Chemicals

The Nuffield Council on Bioethics therefore states quite clearly: "We note, further, that the fact that DNA sequences are essentially just genetic information distinguishes them from other chemical compounds, with regard to the patent system."

In the modern view, a gene is therefore not a precisely defined unit of DNA, but a set of DNA sequences that may recombine continually in a new way and interact in a complex manner with other gene sequences or their environment. It is still not known exactly how the synthesis of several proteins may be induced by one gene. Initial knowledge exists of some mechanisms that lead to this variety of proteins, but it now appears impossible to transform the dynamic and constantly changing set of gene sequences into a patentable object with a precisely defined structure and function. All that is patented is an intellectual construct that has little to do with reality.

An additional factor is that, unlike with chemical substances, it is rarely possible to circumvent a patent on genetic information by inventing a new chemical substance, particularly because the number of human genes is finite. Once these have been analyzed and patented, the blockade effect is much more extensive than in the case of chemical substances, whose number can be constantly increased by means of variations and experimental modifications.

As soon as different patent owners are involved and there is a risk of royalty stacking, research and development are considerably impeded.

The Negative Consequences

The negative consequences also become apparent for small companies that not only sequence genes, but also handle scientifically more complex problems such as gene therapy. Thus, an employee of Mologen [AG] in Berlin has repeatedly voiced public criticism of gene patenting. The company itself has filed numerous patent applications, but fears dependence via patents on genes that are upstream of gene therapy. "Sequencing, the technology by which a gene can be recognized, 'read,' and then patented, has meanwhile become an automated process. Robots, one would think, cannot make inventions, and it should therefore not be possible to patent genes," says Claas Junghans of Mologen AG. In the newspaper "transcript," Junghans also expresses grave reservations about too extensive gene patents: "If we are being asked in 30 years, why the development of a drug against AIDS took so long, then patent law should not be the answer."

Finally, the hasty patenting of human genes really does affect the entire development of drugs and vaccines, which are mainly based on protein technologies. When both are concentrated in one company, as is the case with the large pharma corporations, difficulties can be skimmed over. But as soon as different patent owners are involved and there is a risk of royalty stacking, research and development are considerably impeded. "This could lead to a situation where there will be a need to obtain multiple licenses in order to complete diagnosis. In addition, where a company acquires a bundle of patent rights over different, yet related, aspects of any given invention, the resulting thicket of patents could make further research work difficult as the morass of patents to work around could be perceived to be impenetrable."

Genes Should Not Be Patented

Michael Crichton

Michael Crichton (1942–2008) was a writer and filmmaker, and the author of Next, *a novel that focuses on genetic engineering.*

You, or someone you love, may die because of a gene patent that should never have been granted in the first place. Sound far-fetched? Unfortunately, it's only too real.

The Mistake of Gene Patents

Gene patents are now used to halt research, prevent medical testing and keep vital information from you and your doctor. Gene patents slow the pace of medical advance on deadly diseases. And they raise costs exorbitantly: A test for breast cancer that could be done for $1,000 now costs $3,000.

You can't patent snow, eagles or gravity, and you shouldn't be able to patent genes, either.

Why? Because the holder of the gene patent can charge whatever he wants, and does. Couldn't somebody make a cheaper test? Sure, but the patent holder blocks any competitor's test. He owns the gene. Nobody else can test for it. In fact, you can't even donate your own breast cancer gene to another scientist without permission. The gene may exist in your body, but it's now private property.

This bizarre situation has come to pass because of a mistake by an underfinanced and understaffed government agency. The United States Patent [and Trademark] Office misinterpreted previous Supreme Court rulings and some years ago began—to the surprise of everyone, including scientists decoding the genome—to issue patents on genes.

Michael Crichton, "Patenting Life," *New York Times*, February 13, 2007. Reproduced by permission.

Humans share mostly the same genes. The same genes are found in other animals as well. Our genetic makeup represents the common heritage of all life on earth. You can't patent snow, eagles or gravity, and you shouldn't be able to patent genes, either. Yet by now one-fifth of the genes in your body are privately owned.

The results have been disastrous. Ordinarily, we imagine patents promote innovation, but that's because most patents are granted for human inventions. Genes aren't human inventions, they are features of the natural world. As a result these patents can be used to block innovation, and hurt patient care.

The Effect of Patents on Genetic Tests

For example, Canavan disease is an inherited disorder that affects children starting at 3 months; they cannot crawl or walk, they suffer seizures and eventually become paralyzed and die by adolescence. Formerly there was no test to tell parents if they were at risk. Families enduring the heartbreak of caring for these children engaged a researcher to identify the gene and produce a test. Canavan families around the world donated tissue and money to help this cause.

When the gene was identified in 1993, the families got the commitment of a New York hospital to offer a free test to anyone who wanted it. But the researcher's employer, Miami Children's Hospital Research Institute, patented the gene and refused to allow any health care provider to offer the test without paying a royalty. The parents did not believe genes should be patented and so did not put their names on the patent. Consequently, they had no control over the outcome.

In addition, a gene's owner can in some instances also own the mutations of that gene, and these mutations can be markers for disease. Countries that don't have gene patents actually offer better gene testing than we do, because when multiple labs are allowed to do testing, more mutations are discovered, leading to higher-quality tests.

Apologists for gene patents argue that the issue is a tempest in a teapot, that patent licenses are readily available at minimal cost. That's simply untrue. The owner of the genome for Hepatitis C is paid millions by researchers to study this disease. Not surprisingly, many other researchers choose to study something less expensive.

But forget the costs: Why should people or companies own a disease in the first place? They didn't invent it. Yet today, more than 20 human pathogens are privately owned, including haemophilus influenzae and Hepatitis C. And we've already mentioned that tests for the BRCA genes for breast cancer cost $3,000. Oh, one more thing: If you undergo the test, the company that owns the patent on the gene can keep your tissue and do research on it without asking your permission. Don't like it? Too bad.

The Dangers of Gene Patents

The plain truth is that gene patents aren't benign and never will be. When SARS [severe acute respiratory syndrome] was spreading across the globe, medical researchers hesitated to study it—because of patent concerns. There is no clearer indication that gene patents block innovation, inhibit research and put us all at risk.

Even your doctor can't get relevant information. An asthma medication only works in certain patients. Yet its manufacturer has squelched efforts by others to develop genetic tests that would determine on whom it will and will not work. Such commercial considerations interfere with a great dream. For years we've been promised the coming era of personalized medicine—medicine suited to our particular body makeup. Gene patents destroy that dream.

Fortunately, two congressmen want to make the full benefit of the decoded genome available to us all. Last Friday

[February 9, 2007], Xavier Becerra, a Democrat of California, and Dave Weldon, a Republican of Florida, sponsored the Genomic Research and Accessibility Act [this bill never became law], to ban the practice of patenting genes found in nature. Mr. Becerra has been careful to say the bill does not hamper invention, but rather promotes it. He's right. This bill will fuel innovation, and return our common genetic heritage to us. It deserves our support.

Organizations to Contact

The editors have compiled the following list of organizations concerned with the issues debated in this book. The descriptions are derived from materials provided by the organizations. All have publications or information available for interested readers. The list was compiled on the date of publication of the present volume; the information provided here may change. Be aware that many organizations take several weeks or longer to respond to inquiries, so allow as much time as possible.

American Society of Human Genetics (ASHG)
9650 Rockville Pike, Bethesda, MD 20814-3998
(301) 634-7300 • fax: (301) 634-7079
Web site: www.ashg.org

The American Society of Human Genetics (ASHG) is the primary professional membership organization for human genetics specialists worldwide. ASHG provides forums for advancing genetic research, enhancing genetics education, and promoting responsible scientific policies. ASHG publishes the *American Journal of Human Genetics* and an electronic newsletter *SNP-IT*.

Center for Bioethics & Human Dignity (CBHD)
Trinity International University, 2065 Half Day Road
Deerfield, IL 60015
(847) 317-8180 • fax: (847) 317-8101
e-mail: info@cbhd.org
Web site: www.cbhd.org

The Center for Bioethics & Human Dignity (CBHD) works to bring explicit Christian engagement into the bioethics arena. CBHD seeks to supply leaders with the tools needed to engage the issues of bioethics using rigorous research, conceptual analysis, charitable critique, leading-edge publication, and effective teaching. Reports and podcasts including *Beyond Perfectionism* are available on the center's Web site.

Center for Genetics and Society (CGS)

1936 University Avenue, Suite 350, Berkeley, CA   94704
(510) 625-0819 • fax: (510) 625-0874
e-mail: info@geneticsandsociety.org
Web site: www.geneticsandsociety.org

The Center for Genetics and Society (CGS) is a nonprofit information and public affairs organization working to encourage responsible uses and effective societal governance of the new human genetic and reproductive technologies. CGS works with scientists, health professionals, and civil society leaders to oppose applications of new human genetic and reproductive technologies that objectify and commodify human life and threaten to divide human society. CGS publishes reports, articles, and newsletters, including the report *Playing the Gene Card? A Report on Race and Human Biotechnology.*

Council for Responsible Genetics (CRG)

5 Upland Road, Suite 3, Cambridge, MA   02140
(617) 868-0870 • fax: (617) 491-5344
e-mail: crg@gene-watch.org
Web site: www.councilforresponsiblegenetics.org

Council for Responsible Genetics (CRG) is a nonprofit organization dedicated to fostering public debate about the social, ethical, and environmental implications of genetic technologies. CRG works through the media and concerned citizens to distribute accurate information and represent the public interest on emerging issues in biotechnology. CRG publishes *GeneWatch*, a magazine dedicated to monitoring biotechnology's social, ethical, and environmental consequences.

Ethics and Public Policy Center (EPPC)

1730 M Street NW, Suite 910, Washington, DC   20036
(202) 682-1200 • fax: (202) 408-0632

e-mail: ethics@eppc.org
Web site: www.eppc.org

The Ethics and Public Policy Center (EPPC) is dedicated to applying the Judeo-Christian moral tradition to critical issues of public policy. Through its core programs such as Bioethics and American Democracy, EPPC and its scholars work to influence policy makers and to transform the culture through the world of ideas. EPPC publishes the *New Atlantis*, a quarterly journal about technology with an emphasis on bioethics.

Genetics & Public Policy Center (GPPC)

Johns Hopkins University, Berman Institute of Bioethics
1717 Massachusetts Avenue NW, Suite 530
Washington, DC 20036
(202) 663-5971 • fax: (202) 663-5992
e-mail: gppcnews@jhu.edu
Web site: www.dnapolicy.org

The Genetics & Public Policy Center works to help policy makers, the press, and the public understand the challenges and opportunities of genetic medicine. The center conducts legal research and policy analysis, performs policy-relevant social science research, crafts policy recommendations, and influences national genetics policy. Numerous publications and testimony transcripts, including the report *The Genetic Town Hall: Public Opinion About Research on Genes, Environment, and Health*, are available on the center's Web site.

Institute on Biotechnology & the Human Future (IBHF)

565 West Adams Street, Chicago, IL 60661
(312) 906-5337
e-mail: info@thehumanfuture.org
Web site: www.thehumanfuture.org

The Institute on Biotechnology & the Human Future is a network for exchanging understandings about recent developments in genetics, reproductive technology, and emerging social issues regarding biotechology. IBHF brings together scholars, policy experts, and others to discuss and analyze bio-technologies, including cloning and genetic enhancement. The institute publishes a newsletter and has numerous commentaries on the topic of biotechnology available on its Web site, including *Genism, Racism, and the Prospect of Genetic Genocide.*

National Human Genome Research Institute (NHGRI)
National Institutes of Health, Building 31, Room 4B09
31 Center Drive, MSC 2152, 9000 Rockville Pike
Bethesda, MD   20892-2152
(301) 402-0911 • fax: (301) 402-2218
Web site: www.genome.gov

The National Human Genome Research Institute (NHGRI) led the National Institutes of Health's contribution to the International Human Genome Project. The project's primary goal is the sequencing of the human genome. NHGRI supports the development of resources and technology that will accelerate genome research and its application to human health. NHGRI has many educational tools available on its Web site, including the multimedia *Understanding the Human Genome Project.*

Bibliography

Books

Carol Isaacson Barash — *Just Genes: The Ethics of Genetic Technologies.* Westport, CT: Praeger, 2008.

Roberta M. Berry — *The Ethics of Genetic Engineering.* New York: Routledge, 2007.

Celia Deane-Drummond — *Genetics and Christian Ethics.* New York: Cambridge University Press, 2006.

Joel Garreau — *Radical Evolution: The Promise and Peril of Enhancing Our Minds, Our Bodies—And What It Means to Be Human.* New York: Doubleday, 2005.

Jonathan Glover — *Choosing Children: Genes, Disability, and Design.* New York: Oxford University Press, 2006.

H. Daniel Monsour, ed. — *Ethics and the New Genetics: An Integrated Approach.* Toronto: University of Toronto Press, 2007.

Ramez Naam — *More than Human: Embracing the Promise of Biological Enhancement.* New York: Broadway Books, 2005.

Erik Parens, Audrey R. Chapman, and Nancy Press, eds. — *Wrestling with Behavioral Genetics: Science, Ethics, and Public Conversation.* Baltimore, MD: Johns Hopkins University Press, 2006.

Michael J. Sandel — *The Case Against Perfection: Ethics in the Age of Genetic Engineering.* Cambridge, MA: Belknap Press, 2007.

Julian Savulescu and Nick Bostrom, eds. — *Human Enhancement.* New York: Oxford University Press, 2009.

Pete Shanks — *Human Genetic Engineering: A Guide for Activists, Skeptics, and the Very Perplexed.* New York: Nation Books, 2005.

Thomas A. Shannon, ed. — *Genetics: Science, Ethics, and Public Policy: A Reader.* Lanham, MD: Rowman & Littlefield, 2005.

Neil F. Sharpe and Ronald F. Carter — *Genetic Testing: Care, Consent, and Liability.* Hoboken, NJ: Wiley-Liss, 2006.

Claudio M. Tamburrini and Torbjörn Tännsjö — *Genetic Technology and Sport: Ethical Questions.* New York: Routledge, 2005.

Ronnee K. Yashon and Michael R. Cummings — *Human Genetics and Society.* Belmont, CA: Brooks/Cole, 2009.

Simon Young — *Designer Evolution: A Transhumanist Manifesto.* Amherst, NY: Prometheus Books, 2006.

Periodicals

Bryan Appleyard — "Design Fault," *Spectator*, March 4, 2006.

Rebecca Atkinson   "I Wouldn't Have Minded If My Baby Had Been Born Deaf, but the Embryology Bill Insists I Should," *Guardian*, October 10, 2008.

Ronald Bailey   "Human Rights and Human Enhancement: Is Genetic Modification of People Moral?" *Reason Online*, May 29, 2006. www.reason.com.

Susannah Baruch and Kathy L. Hudson   "Civilian and Military Genetics: Nondiscrimination Policy in a Post-GINA World," *American Journal of Human Genetics*, October 2008.

Marcy Darnovsky   "Red Flags over Consumer Genetics," *San Diego Union Tribune*, May 22, 2008.

Economist   "Owning the Body and the Soul," March 12, 2005.

Masha Gessen   "Jewish Guinea Pigs: What if a Gene Patent Is Bad for the Jews," *Slate*, July 26, 2005. www.slate.com.

Denise Grady   "Girl or Boy? As Fertility Technology Advances, so Does an Ethical Debate," *New York Times*, February 6, 2007.

Henry Greely   "The Genetics of Fear," *Democracy: A Journal of Ideas*, Spring 2008. www.democracyjournal.org.

Amy Harmon   "Prenatal Test Puts Down Syndrome in Hard Focus," *New York Times*, May 9, 2007.

Kathy L. Hudson, M.K. Holohan, and Francis S. Collins — "Keeping Pace with the Times—The Genetic Information Nondiscrimination Act of 2008," *New England Journal of Medicine*, June 19, 2008.

Andrew J. Imparato and Anne C. Sommers — "ADA and the New Eugenics," *Washington Examiner*, August 10, 2005.

Claudia Kalb — "Peering into the Future," *Newsweek*, December 11, 2006.

Sara Katsanis and Gail H. Javitt — "Surreptitious DNA Testing," Genetics & Public Policy Center, January 2009. www.dnapolicy.org.

David King — "The Human Fertilisation and Embryology Bill 2008," Center for Genetics and Society, April 15, 2009. www.geneticsandsociety.org.

William Saletan — "Leave This Child Behind: Sports, Segregation, and Environmental Eugenics," *Slate*, December 1, 2008. www.slate.com.

Darshak M. Sanghavi — "Wanting Babies Like Themselves, Some Parents Choose Genetic Defects," *New York Times*, December 5, 2006.

Scientific American — "The Need to Regulate 'Designer Babies,'" May 2009.

Wesley J. Smith — "Politically Correct Eugenics: Brownback and Kennedy Do the Right Thing," *Weekly Standard*, March 31, 2008.

Rob Stein   "New Safety, New Concerns in Tests for Down Syndrome," *Washington Post*, February 24, 2009.

Beth Whitehouse   "Experts Fear Potential Abuses of Genetic Screening," *Newsday*, July 18, 2008.

George F. Will   "Will: The Attack on Kids with Down Syndrome," *Newsweek*, January 29, 2007.

Cathy Young   "A Guide for the Modern Prometheus: Is There a Right Way to Transcend Biology?" *Reason Online*, July 11, 2006. www.reason.com.

Andi Zeisler and Emily Galpern   "Conceiving the Future: Reproductive-Justice Activists on Technology and Policy," *Bitch*, June 6, 2008.

Index